American Film Acting
The Stanislavski Heritage

Studies in Cinema, No. 28

Diane M. Kirkpatrick, Series Editor

Professor, History of Art
The University of Michigan

Other Titles in This Series

American Film Acting
The Stanislavski Heritage

by
Richard A. Blum

UMI RESEARCH PRESS
Ann Arbor, Michigan

Burgess
PN
1995
.B4978
1984

Produced and distributed by
UMI Research Press
an imprint of
University Microfilms International
A Xerox Information Resources Company
Ann Arbor, Michigan 48106

Library of Congress Cataloging in Publication Data

Blum, Richard A.
 American film acting.

 (Studies in cinema ; no. 28)
 Revision of thesis—University of Southern
California, 1977.
 Bibliography: p.
 Includes index.
 1. Moving-picture acting. 2. Stanislavsky method.
3. Moving-pictures—United States—History. I. Title.
II. Series.
PN1995.B4978 1984   791.43'028   84-8778
ISBN 0-8357-1609-0 (pbk. : alk. paper)
ISBN 0-8357-1590-6 (case)

For Jason and Jennifer

A time will come when the evolution of art shall have completed its predestined circle and nature itself will teach us methods and techniques for the interpretation of the sharpness of the new life.

—C. Stanislavski, *My Life in Art*

The intimacy of acting of the Stanislavski school... is inevitably and remarkably developed in the cinema.

—V.I. Pudovkin, *Film Acting: A Course of Lectures Delivered at the State Institute of Cinematography, Moscow*

[Method] actors made a powerful impression and showed a remarkable ability to bridge the gap between stage, screen, and television to an extent that aroused excitement and interest in the rest of the world.

—Lee Strasberg, "Acting," in the *New Encyclopaedia Britannica*

Contents

Acknowledgments

I would like to thank all the historians and professionals who contributed in so many ways to the completion of this book. I appreciate the thoughtful comments and feedback offered throughout the various stages of research and manuscript preparation.

During the research phases, I received a great deal of support and assistance from staff members at theatre libraries and special collections, including the University of Southern California, the University of Texas Theatre Collection, the New York Public Library Theatre Collection, and the American Film Institute Resource Center. The Actors Studio in New York and Los Angeles provided considerable assistance in compiling information about the history of the Studio and its impact on film.

Interviews with professionals in the field, and with scholars in theatre and film studies, provided valuable advice which has been incorporated into the body of the text.

For permission to reprint materials in the book, I would like to thank the Billy Rose Theatre Collection/Lincoln Center for the Performing Arts, Museum of Modern Art/Film Still Archives, American Film Institute Still Collection, and the Speech Communication Association of America.

I am particularly grateful to my family for their patience, understanding and support during the long stages of manuscript preparation. For this, the book is dedicated to them.

Introduction

Constantin Stanislavski (1863-1938) was one of Russia's most prominent theatre directors. At the turn of the century, he founded the Moscow Art Theatre specifically to work on techiques of achieving realistic acting. The system he evolved had enormous impact on world theatre, with directors, actors, and teachers interpreting the system in a diversity of ways. One of the most controversial interpretations of the system evolved in America, with the teachings of the American Lab Theatre in the twenties, the Group Theatre in the thirties, and the Actors Studio in the ensuing years. These became fundamental training grounds for actors and directors in theatre and film.

Many books have been written about Stanislavski and his influence on European and American theatre. However, none of those books examined the very real impact the system has had on American film acting. This book provides an overview of the historical impact of the system, and shows how the system has been absorbed into the mainstream of American film.

Early Works on Stage and Screen Acting

The influence of Stanislavski on stage has been documented in works such as Christine Edwards' *The Stanislavski Heritage: Its Contribution to the Russian and American Theatre* (1965). This valuable study provided a thorough overview of the system in Moscow and America, but did not relate the system to any aspect of American film acting. In fact, it ignored the cinema as a developing art form.

The dual development of theatre and film was investigated by A. Nicholas Vardac in *Stage to Screen* (1949, rpt. 1968). The text traced the rise of pictorial realism on the nineteenth-century stage, beginning with Garrick on stage and extending through Griffith on film. Vardac contended that the vogue for pictorial realism in theatre ultimately gave rise to cinematic realism. Although he considered the acting styles of Irving, Belasco, and McKaye, he did not deal with the experimentation of Stanislavski and the Moscow Art Theatre, nor with the transition of acting styles from stage to screen.

Other scholars have isolated acting as a singular art form, also concentrating primarily on theatre. Edwin Duerr's *Length and Depth of Acting* (1962) provided scholarly insight into historical acting styles throughout the world, but did not emphasize cinematic acting requirements. In *A History of American Acting* (1966), Garff Wilson presented an overview of theatrical acting styles and techniques, but provided minimal insight into evolving film styles in this country. Toby Cole and Helen Chinoy offered a wide compendium of views on world acting in *Actors on Acting* (rev. ed., 1970), but minimized discussion of film acting requirements and aesthetics.

A number of books and articles have been devoted to specific techniques of acting, but these, too, fail to consider common derivations or interrelationships. They typically fall into the category of acting for theatre *or* acting for film. Most works view the two arts as separate and distinct.

In the early days of film, for example, many works appeared that stressed physicality of form and behavior as the unique requirements of film acting. Such works included Frances Agnew's *Motion Picture Acting* (1913), Mae Marsh's *Screen Acting* (1921), Inez and Helen Klumph's *Screen Acting: Its Requirements and Rewards* (1922), which was used as a supplementary text in the New York Institute of Photography, Agnes Platt's *Practical Hints on Acting for the Cinema* (1923), the *Paramount Picture School Catalogue* (1925), and *Cinema: Practical Courses in Cinema Acting in Ten Complete Lessons* (n.d.), with writings by Mary Pickford and others.

Similarly, works on stage acting never acknowledged film as a contemporary art form. They typically stressed techniques of theatrical "inspiration" as the foundation for stage performance. These works included F.F. Mackay's *The Art of Acting* (1913), William Gillette's *The Illusion of the First Time* (1913), Brander Matthew's *On Acting* (1914), Arthur Hornblow's *Training for the Stage* (1916), Mrs. Fiske's *Her Views on Actors, Acting, and the Problems of Production* (1917), and Dion Boucicault's *The Art of Acting* (1926).

The fact was ignored that cinema and theatre shared artistic roots. Lewis Jacobs, in his classic study, *The Rise of the American Film* (1939), detailed the phases of early cinematic growth. The initial phase was actually based on stage plays photographed intact, with the camera providing the audience perspective. The second phase of development was extremely exaggerated pantomime, a lateral step from the pantomime training which many stage actors received. The final phase began with D.W. Griffith who sought the same kind of realism on screen that Stanislavski sought on stage. Although Griffith was a stage actor for many years, he preferred to hire actors with no stage training, contending that the requirements of the media are disparate; an actor "has a much better chance in pictures if he has never been on the stage."[1]

During that early period of film, other important theatre professionals and critics—including Daniel Frohman, David Belasco, Brander Matthews,

Otis Skinner, and Bernard Shaw—wrote on the artistic conflict between theatre and film. The consensus appeared to be that two different media were in coexistence, each with its own techniques and requirements.

In the 1930s through the 1940s, when the Group Theatre was popularizing the emotional realities of the Stanislavski system for the stage, V.I. Pudovkin related his theories of the cinema in *Film Technique and Film Acting* (published collectively in 1954). Pudovkin contended that the technical requirements of cinema outmoded the traditional conventions of the stage. The necessary attributes of theatre acting—such as voice projection, exaggerated diction, theatricalized movements, stylized make-up, and so on—were unnecessary and distracting in cinema. Film required a new sense of intimacy and naturalism.

Pudovkin recognized that Stanislavski was limited by the conventions of the theatre. He felt that Stanislavski's ideas could not fully be realized until the development of the cinematic process. Stanislavski sought "gestureless" moments, for example, in which the actor was totally concentrated; Pudovkin claimed this was impossible for theatre, but was natural and essential for film:

> It is amazing that [the] solution of this very problem is not only *not* impracticable in the cinema, but extreme paucity of gesture, often literal immobility, is absolutely indispensable in it.[2]

In short, Pudovkin felt that Stanislavski's approach to acting came closest to the actual needs of film actors, particularly in the realm of emotional "absorption," which can be distinguished from theatricality for the stage. The adaptation of Stanislavski precepts for the screen would involve an initial separation of theatrical conventionality from emotional truthfulness.

A number of important American critics of the thirties and forties discussed the parallelism of theatre and film from an aesthetic perspective. Writers such as Stark Young, Allardyce Nicoll, John Andersen, and Harold Stearns tended to define the large screen as a more realistic medium than the live theatre. William K. Howard went so far as to claim that film and theatre acting were virtually the same.[3]

As Russian films came into America with nonactors in lead roles, a new controversy arose over the necessity of training actors for the screen. Did typecasting deny the necessity for an acting system, or was personal "behaving" sufficient and desirable for the actor on screen? The issue was considered at length by Pudovkin and Sergei Eisenstein, and was debated in articles such as Alice Brady, "The Problem of Casting by Type" (1929); Edith Isaacs, "Type Casting: Eighth Deadly Sin" (1933); and Irving Pichel, "Character, Personality and Image: A Note on Screen Acting" (1946). In "Acting and Behaving" (1946), Alexander Knox tried to counter the prevailing attitude that technique is valuable only to the theatre, while "behaving" is essential to film. He defined behaving as "a form of acting which is much admired in Hollywood and elsewhere, mainly on the grounds that it holds the mirror up to nature."[4] That attitude was indicative of a misunderstanding about the goals of the Method in American acting, and is still prevalent today. The critical result has been an inherent preference for either the Hollywood star who plays himself, or for the nonprofessional who is cast by type to "be" himself.[5]

The problem of "being" versus "developing a character" peaked in the fifties and sixties, when the Method became the most prominent and controversial style of acting in America. Suddenly works appeared that tried to clarify the system as practiced at the Actors Studio, from the "authentic" system as embodied in Stanislavski's trilogy: *An Actor Prepares* (1936), *Building a Character* (1949), and *Creating a Role* (1961). In succession, those works included Robert Lewis's *Method or Madness?* (1958), E.R. Hapgood's *Stanislavski Legacy* (1959), Sonia Moore's *The Stanislavski Method* (1960), later revised as *The Stanislavski System* (1965, 1974); Robert Hethmon's *Strasberg at the Actors Studio: Tape Recorded Sessions* (1965), and Edward Easty's *On Method Acting* (1966).

About the same time the Method was absorbed into the mainstream of theatre and film, a number of European theories of acting affected the American stage. The bulk of theatre remained realistic, but a significant movement away from realism was inspired by Antonin Artaud's *Theatre and Its Double* (English translation, 1958), Michel St. Denis' *Theatre: The Rediscovery of Style* (1960), John Willet's *Brecht on Theatre* (1964), and Jerzy Grotowski's *Toward a Poor Theatre* (1968).

Actors who were trained in the Method were ideally suited for the traditional stage and the intimate requirements of motion picture acting. In the latter part of the century, training for motion pictures became synonymous with the Method school of the Actors Studio. The most definitive work on the history of the Actors Studio remains David Garfield's *A Player's Place* (1980). This book carefully and objectively analyzed the historical dimensions of the Studio, its techniques, and its prime players. With actors trained in variations of the Stanislavski system, branching out from the Actors Studio and other experimental forums, screen acting became a natural extension of Stanislavski's search for realism.

1

Background

Stanislavski's Search for Realism

Constantin Sergeevich Stanislavski (Konstantin Sergeevich Alekseev) sought the ultimate in acting realism for his performers, but felt restricted by the physical limitations of the stage. These limitations led him to consider the use of cinema for acting training:

> The impossibility of repeating the impression received by the spectator limits the role of the theatre as a place for the study of the art of the stage... It would be possible, what with the present state of perfected invention, to try to enter the voices of dramatic artists on phonograph records, and their gestures and mimics on the films of the cinema and this would give a great deal of help to young actors.[1]

In his autobiography, *My Life in Art* (1924), he recounted an incident that had direct bearing upon his desire to achieve ultimate realism. While touring Kiev, he found himself in a beautifully landscaped palace park, reminiscent of a setting in Turgenev's *A Month in the Country*. He began improvising the scene with his actors, utilizing the entire surroundings: a long alley path, ancient flower beds, summerhouses, benches. Yet he stopped the scene in mid-action "because I could not continue my false and theatrical pose. All that I had done seemed untrue to nature, to reality. And it had been said of us that we had developed simplicity to a point of naturalism!"[2]

The incident was unsettling for him. In a realistic setting, Stanislavski could not be natural; in a theatrical setting, where scenic truth was not real, he could perform appropriately through stage conventions. Stanislavski apparently glimpsed the kind of truth that might be accessible in film:

> The trees, the air, the sun hinted to us of such real, beautiful and artistic truth which cannot, because of its aestheticism, be compared to that which is created in us by the dead wings of the theatre.... This artistic truth, hinted to us by nature, is incomparably more aesthetic and more beautiful and what is even more important, more scenic than the relative truth and theatrical conventionality with which it is the habit to limit theatrical effectiveness.[3]

At the conclusion of his memoirs, Stanislavski wrote: "The only king and ruler of the stage is the talented actor. But alas, I cannot find for him a true scenic background which would not interfere with, but help his complex spiritual work."[4] Still, he was not prepared to accept cinema as the answer to his creative needs. He felt an intense rivalry between the stage and film, and considered films to be commercially dominated, with little regard for artistic concerns. In a letter to Firmin Gemier, dated April 1926, Stanislavski bemoaned the state of world theatre, and attacked the commercialism of stage and film:

> Weakened at first by the cinema, and later beaten by the war, the theatre is compelled to serve the very bad taste of the newly arisen elements who possess capital, a special class of profiteers who inundate the capitals of all countries and set the tune. The modern repertoire and modern productions adapt themselves mostly to their taste. Extravagant productions and the tinselly wealth of breathtaking hokum with nude women and sordid plots, much like the cinema's, are staged for them.[5]

In January 1933, five years before his death, Stanislavski wrote in an address for his seventieth birthday celebration:

> When we think of the future [of theatre] and our dangerous rival, the cinema, we perceive the unhappy fate that lies in store for all the bad theatres in the world. They will have to give up their place to the cinema, which has begun to speak too loudly...For all this, I see a rosy future for the theatre. There will be fewer theatres, but those that survive will be splendid, imbued with genuine art, and genuine art springs from the laws of creative nature.[6]

A genuine art of acting seemed impossible in a commercially dominated medium, which is precisely why Stanislavski cofounded the Moscow Art Theatre (M.A.T.) in 1897, with Vladimir Nemirovich-Danchenko. Stanislavski's experiments in acting were motivated by the desire to bring "inner truth" to the stage, which was then dominated by pictorial display and declamatory acting:

> We protested against the customary manner of acting, against theatricality, against pathos, against declamation, against overacting, against the bad manner of production, against the habitual scenery, against the star system which spoiled the ensemble, against the light and farcical repertoire which was being cultivated on the Russian stage....Then, as well as now [1924] we sought for inner truth.[7]

Stanislavski was not rejecting the traditions of the stage, so much as modifying and unifying them. He was influenced by Saxe-Meiningen's concepts of the acting ensemble, and the creation of specific lines of action for each character on stage.[8] He sought to implement similar goals. The theatre he wanted to change was marked by pictorialism, romanticism, and the peak of the star system, just as it was in America. One critic perceptively noted that Stanislavski "can be identified historically as the man who amalgamated the established technique of theatre with the emotional intensity of erratic nineteenth century actors."[9]

Stanislavski had been experimenting with various emotional and physical means of achieving a sense of inner truth on stage, and his actors finally "grew angry and said that I was transforming the rehearsals into the efforts of an experimentalist, that actors were not guinea pigs...."[10] The first draft of his system, delineating the basic concepts and exercises, became available for Moscow Art Theatre members in 1909.[11] Two years later, Stanislavski formed the First Studio, supervised by Leopold Sulerzhitski to test and develop his system of behavioral realism. His students included Eugene Vakhtangov, Richard Boleslavski, Vera Soloviova, and Michael Chekhov, each of whom interpreted Stanislavski in a different way, and contributed to the American understanding of the system.

The System Defined

Stanislavski's experiments were designed to find means of controlling the erratic nature of emotions, imagination, and spontaneity. This concept of control was crucial to the idea of a trained artist:

> The main difference between the art of the actor and all other arts is that every other artist may create whenever he is in the mood of inspiration. But the artist of the stage must be the master of his own inspiration and must know how to call it forth when it is announced on the posters of the theatre. This is the chief secret of our art.[12]

His experimentation with creative control was based on his observation of actors who seemed "natural" on stage. He found they had several characteristics in common: they seemed relaxed and free of muscular tension; they seemed concentrated on the objects of performance; they seemed to control emotions by "prodding" rather than forcing responses. In essence, these three observations, coupled with an emphasis upon voice, face, and body, became the principle guidelines of the evolving system.[13]

The system itself was not comprised of a set of rules or formulae, but rather a number of experimental steps that might lead to the "true" creative state in performance, that is, the state of a normal person in everyday life. At the First Studio, Stanislavski experimented with different techniques to achieve the true creative state at will, including improvisations, sense memory, relaxation and concentration, emotional memory, and the analysis of play structure and content.[14] The M.A.T. actors were the first to have a systematic framework for approaching the character and the script, on both emotional and physical planes.

The system offered a new psychological foundation for understanding character and action. The given circumstances of a play, motivations of the character, and intentions of the scene were examined in depth. The play was systematically and comprehensively broken down into the author's thematic objective ("superobjective"), units of dramatic action ("beats"), and throughlines of action for the character. For the first time in acting history, the approach to character and theme were intricately and psychologically interwoven.

Using psychological reality as a baseline, Stanislavski experimented with emotional memory to achieve a sense of inner truth. His work on emotional memory was extensive, and was later misconstrued as the most important element of the training process. The concept of using personal feeling in acting was not new; it dated back to Talma's "Reflections on Acting" (1877), which advocated using emotions "as if they were [the actor's] own."[15] Stanislavski, however, provided a specific means for achieving that goal. Emotional memory exercises provided the stimulus for recalling "those feelings which are beyond the reach of the conscious mind."[16] The concept was patterned after the principles outlined by Theodore Ribot in *The Psychology of Emotions* (1897), and was fully developed by Stanislavski in 1914.

The emotional realm of training was only one aspect of the actor's art. It is clear that Stanislavski meant the actor to be disciplined in both external and inner techniques:

> Parallel with [inner technique] development should go the development of an external technique—the perfecting of a physical apparatus which serves to incarnate the stage image created by the actor for his part, and also express in precise and vivid ways the inner life of the character.[17]

After several more years of experimentation, Stanislavski actually reversed his emphasis on inner technique, and concluded that the logic of physical actions provided a greater access to truth on stage. In the thirties, he virtually abandoned the idea of emotional memory as a vital tool for expressing reality.[18] Much of his later work, however, went unnoticed in America, and his emphasis on physical training was largely ignored. Lee Strasberg, who cofounded the Group Theatre and became artistic director of the Actors Studio, concluded: "We would never get on with the business of acting" if the physical sphere of training were incorporated into the Method.[19] In America, the emotional aspects of the system dominated all other aspects.

America's Interpretation of the System

The practitioners of the system in America learned the early version of Stanislavski's work, primarily through the efforts of Boleslavski and his American Laboratory Theatre in 1923. Boleslavski, a director-member of the M.A.T., offered America its first published account of the system in

"Stanislavski—The Man and His Methods," published in *Theatre Magazine* (April 1923). In addition, he published six lessons in acting, surveying the different facets of the early system; the works were published collectively as *Acting: The First Six Lessons* (1949), and had a significant impact on acting training in this country.

Boleslavski's work at the lab inspired two major figures who helped create the Group Theatre in the 1930s. Lee Strasberg and Harold Clurman followed the tradition of sensory technique, adding a new emphasis on the analytic search for inner truth. The Group Theatre's stress on inner technique as the key to Stanislavski's teachings was reinforced by the American publication of Stanislavski's *An Actor Prepares* (1936), which reflected his initial concern with emotional and psychological truth in acting. Stanislavski's second book, *Building a Character* (1949) conveyed the importance of physicalization but had little impact on theatre or film, since the modified version, known as the Method, was already established as the standard for serious American acting. Stanislavski's sequel, *Creating a Role* (1961), emphasized external technique but was published too late to offset the analytical approach in America. By mid-century, American theatre and film acting styles centered on the psychoanalytical underpinnings developed in Strasberg's work at the Actor's Studio.

In contrast to the Actors Studio emphasis on internal and analytical action, a number of works appeared at mid-century, re-emphasizing Stanislavski's concern with physicalized action. Michael Chekhov, for example, stressed the idea of inspiration and psychological gesture in *To the Actor* (1953). His book was followed by Nicolai Gorchakov's *Stanislavski Directs* (1954), which had a critical impact since it was based on original M.A.T. class notes. Here Stanislavski asserted that the system he devised was meant to be "the means for the realistic embodiment of the dramatist's ideas,"[20] it was not meant to be an end in itself.

The conflict over the "true" interpretation of Stanislavski peaked in the fifties and sixties, when the Actors Studio dominated stage and film. Cofounder of the studio, Robert Lewis, presented a series of lectures, collectively published as *Method or Madness?* (1958), to clarify Stanislavski's own ideas for the American actor. It was an exceedingly valuable text in that respect. A few years later, *The Tulane Drama Review* (Fall and Winter, 1964) published two special issues devoted to the uses and theories of Stanislavski in America, offering a perspective on different modifications of the system, with charges and countercharges, interviews and debates. In 1966, Lee Strasberg belatedly and heatedly defended his Method approach in an article addressed directly to *The Tulane Drama Review* inquiry.[21]

Sonia Moore, who studied at the M.A.T., published *The Stanislavski System* (1965, 1974), two revised editions of an earlier work, to reflect Stanislavski's later emphasis on the unity of physical and psychological realities. She carefully explained Stanislavski's method of physical actions, and provided a thorough understanding of the system as it evolved. Still, the debates continued erratically throughout the decade[22].

In Moscow, the system was flexible enough to provide the impetus for experimental use by directors such as Meyerhold and Vakhtangov, both of whom had a great impact on Lee Strasberg in later years (along with Gordon Craig). Vsevold Meyerhold experimented with directorial symbols and images rather than with actors' problems of performance.[23] Eugene Vakhtangov experimented with theatrical imagery, often through improvisation, to achieve a blend of inner truth *and* theatrical truth.[24] Stanislavski observed and admired that experimentation, claiming that Vakhtangov had discovered a powerful new use for the system.[25]

In America, the system was viewed more narrowly, particularly by Strasberg and the proponents of the Method school. Their psychoanalytic interpretation of the system dominated late twentieth-century acting styles, and provided a workable technique for the continuing demands of realistic acting on stage, film, and television.

Paving the Way for the System: American Stage and Screen Acting, 1900-1930s

The Pictorial Theatre

Stanislavski created the Moscow Art Theatre (M.A.T.) in response to the commercial domination of the stage. In America, a similar revolt occurred. Throughout the early twentieth century, art theatres sprang up in opposition to theatrical commercialism. The Provincetown Theatre (which launched Eugene O'Neill) was created with the avowed purpose of not "submitting to the commercial manager's interpretation of public taste."[1] The Neighborhood Playhouse was organized to counter the "photographic representation [which] dominated the commercial stage."[2] The Washington Square Players, which eventually became the Theatre Guild, patterned itself after the M.A.T.'s approach to dramatic honesty and stylistic vision.[3]

Although art theatres were founded across America, the mainstream of theatre appealed to the public taste for pictorial display. Producers and audiences sought detailed realism in stage pictures, rather than the behavioral realism of acting. As Vardac suggests, "unlike the realism of the Moscow Art Theatre or the Theatre Libre of Antoine, this type of pictorial setting was the chief actor in the play, attracting attention to itself."[4]

David Belasco was, perhaps, the American master of intricate and spectacular staging of popular romantic and melodramatic plays. In *The Girl of the West* (1905), starring Blanche Bates and Frank Keenan, he created a startlingly effective blizzard. In *The Easiest Way* (1909), he used a room from an actual boarding house, complete with accessories and original wallpaper. In *The Governor's Child* (1912) he created a replica of the popular Child's Restaurant, which served food and drink to the actors on stage.

Belasco was not only concerned about the realism of the sets, but about the observable realism of performers. He wanted to provide a proper atmosphere for creative functioning and felt free to experiment accordingly. When he produced a Japanese spectacular called *The Darling of the Gods* (1902), he rehearsed his actors in kimonos and Japanese footwear to familiarize them with the costumes. Stanislavski used similar experimental techniques, rehearsing his actors in togas and cloaks to familiarize them with period costumes for *Julius Caesar* (1903)[5]. Both men sought to establish a realistic framework and orientation for their actors in the realization of their roles. Daniel Frohman, a contemporary of Belasco's, referred to him as a manager with "an instinctive, almost uncanny feeling for drama.... He would rehearse... until he was satisfied that it rang true."[6]

Since the theatrical focus was on pictorial display, it is not surprising that many American actors were concerned primarily with the physicalization of emotions, that is, the outward appearance of emotions.[7] An indication of the prevailing attitude was expressed by F.F. MacKay, who asserted that acting is formally constituted by the "premeditated use of those forms of voice, pose, and gesture by which emotions are generally expressed in nature."[8]

Throughout the first quarter of the century, more realistic experimentation occurred, and acting tended to move in the general direction of "inner" work. Joseph Jefferson reported he acted best "when the heart is warm and the head cool."[9] Richard Mansfield, like Stanislavski, felt that identification with a part should be so intense that the actor on stage "merge himself in the character he presents."[10] Mansfield, in essence, predated the Actors Studio vogue of the 1950s, which capitalized on the psychoanalytic merger of self and character. William Gillette, who popularized the concept of the "illusion of the first time in acting,"[11] sought a controlled sense of spontaneity in performance. Like Stanislavski, Louis Calvert wanted to develop an actor's ability to control emotions and master his creative resources;[12] he came closest to establishing an emotionally-oriented style for American actors.

Minnie Maddern Fiske, one of the most prominent actresses of the American stage, also helped shift the emphasis toward more emotional control. She sought a scientific approach to recapturing emotions at will, and portraying them through the logic of physical actions: "Anyone may achieve on some rare occasion an outburst of genuine feeling, a gesture of imperishable beauty; a ringing accent of truth; but your scientific actor knows how he did it. He can repeat it again."[13] Her experimentation was much like Stanislavski's, whose entire system was based on the need to provided a means for controlling emotion, creativity, and spontaneity. Both theatrical experimenters stressed the importance of strengthening the actor's imagination and concentration; they similarly stressed vocal training and physical work. As for observation, Mrs. Fiske recommended the actor explore the world around him, with full perception and awareness: "Go where you can find something fresh to bring back to the stage."[14] Stanislavski recommended the actor "study the life and psychology of the people who surround him... both at home and abroad."[15]

In short, most popular acting at the turn of the century was pictorial in nature, but experimentation by individual actors and managers was shifting the aesthetic to a more intimate style.

David Belasco Experiments

By 1911, David Belasco made a substantial departure from pictorial emphasis when he declared he was convinced that " 'action' on the stage is wholly mental and not at all physical."[16] Several factors contributed to this more realistic experimentation: the star system was gradually being replaced by the ensemble approach; plays were being written in psychologically realistic style; settings were becoming more intimate; acting styles were concurrently being refined. The transition was quite evident by 1913, when Belasco wrote:

> Stage traditions were good enough for awhile till the audience outgrew them. One day the heroine who used to shout her grief till the gallery shook found no sympathy with her audiences.... This sort of emotional display became too unreal...so the ranting heroine of melodrama was banished from the stage.[17]

Like the Stanislavski actor, the Belasco actor no longer engaged in an excessive amount of stage business and physicalized action. Rather, his blocking was now related to given circumstances of the play itself. He was concerned with physical actions as they derived from the reality of the scene. By 1921, Belasco was seeking a means of controlling the imaginative aspects of the actor's art. Sounding very much like Mrs. Fiske, Louis Calvert, and Stanislavski, he wrote:

> To wait, in acting, for inspiration to flash upon you is about as sensible as to wait until your house is in flames before looking for a fire escape. Night after night...the same words must be spoken, the same actions to be performed in the same way, in order to produce the same effects upon audiences which continually vary.[18]

Belasco now felt that imagination, coupled with sensitivity and intelligence, was the key to conveying feelings. Acting was becoming an art and a science.

The Belasco experimentation stopped short of allowing emotional and personal feelings to intrude on acting. The scientific regulation of acting meant the ability to convey the illusion of emotions, without experiencing the actual emotions. In this sense, he contrasted strongly with the Stanislavski approach, which required the use of emotional and physical techniques to achieve inner truth in character. Belasco was also opposed to the goal of absolute truth on stage, asserting that "no way to failure in acting is so pure and so short as that of attempting to hold up nature itself instead of the picture or reflection of Nature."[19]

After the M.A.T. and Stanislavski arrived in New York in 1923, Belasco totally reversed his stance. Stanislavski and his troupe provided a visual model for inner truth on stage, which Belasco adopted for his own actors. He now expressed an abiding concern for authentic performances in natural settings, and sought a total commitment to the inner and outer life of the character portrayed.[20] In 1924, Stanislavski publicly commended Belasco's experimentation for "the same atmosphere, attention, and care, and the same devotion to theatre which are the heart and soul of our home stage."[21] Three years later, he made Belasco an honorary member of the M.A.T., lauding his dedication to the precepts of psychological realism on stage. Belasco responded with this letter:

July 23, 1927

Dear Mr. Stanislavski:

Morris Gest has given to me the precious medal and papers telling of the honour the Moscow Art Theatre has done me. Nothing could give me quite as much pleasure and pride as being a member of that organization of great artists whose fame is world wide and who brought to my country a knowledge of the superb art of yours.

I know that your personal efforts did much towards procuring this honour for me and I thank you with all my heart....

Cordially and with deep and sincere regards and admiration, I am dear M. Stanislavski

Faithfully,

David Belasco[22]

Belasco's emphasis on acting was not oriented toward the same kind of artistic goals and techniques as the M.A.T. players. The Belasco sense of realistic detail coupled with understated acting influenced the course of American acting. That influence extended beyond the stage, into film with men like D.W. Griffith, known as the "Belasco of films,"[23] and C.B. DeMille, who carried Belasco theory directly into the cinema.[24]

Silent Film Acting

The theatre audiences were used to Belasco melodramas and spectacles, and the emerging cinema became a natural extension of that aesthetic taste. As Vardac suggests:

Audiences immediately identified the cinema from its first showings, with the nineteenth century vogue of pictorial theatre. It was readily established as the most realistic medium yet available to the theatrical arts. The stage might represent reality, but the motion picture could photograph it.[25]

For the most part, film acting at the turn of the century was considered a craft separate and distinct from stage acting. It required only physical skills coupled with broad movements and gestures. Actors were more concerned with physical stunts and blocking than with character analysis. Lewis Jacobs categorized the early conventions of film acting that mitigated against any serious approach to characterization: all physical business was highly exaggerated; speeches were "mouthed" broadly and unnaturally; action had to take place in horizontal blocking patterns (films were shot like photographed stage plays); the actor had to face the camera at all times; entrances and exits were mandatory for all scenes.[26] In short, the actor was subject to a number of conventions that de-emphasized any need for inner realism or depth of character.

Stage actors from the Belasco stage and the developing art theatres dismissed film as a nonacting medium. It could not compete with the stage for creative challenge, prestige, or even recognition (no screen credits were provided). Film producers, consequently, had difficulty finding dependable actors, or enticing theatre actors to try the new medium. One of the companies, Vitagraph Studio, attempted to solve the problem by forming a stock company with two strong incentives: "steady work and a regular salary of twenty to forty dollars a week."[27] In practice, the "steady work" became propmaking, scene construction, costume sewing, and similar tasks. Film actors complained about their exploitation, but had no bargaining power at the studios. It was not until the star system evolved that they achieved some degree of prestige.

In theatre, the regisseur (producer-director) developed his own stars and exploited their names on the marquee. In film, however, the actor remained anonymous until Carl Laemmle, head of the independent film company IMP, created his own star. He hired Florence Lawrence, formerly known as "The Biograph Girl," and published a false account of her death, stating that she was the victim of a streetcar accident in St. Louis. He then took out an indignant advertisement that proclaimed she was very much alive:

> Miss Lawrence was not even in a streetcar accident, is in the best of health, will continue to appear in "Imp" Films, and very shortly some of the best work in her career is to be released. We now announce our next films.... [28]

A subsequent advertisement proclaimed that Miss Lawrence would allay all fears by visiting St. Louis in person, along with King Baggott, her leading man. The public's excitement over the motion picture star was successfully piqued.[29] Other independent companies were quick to exploit the values of promotion and stardom, and eventually the major companies yielded to the pressure for actor recognition. The star system was established by 1913; the film actor was fast becoming the new focal point of attention.

About the same time the star system developed in film, the Famous Players Film Company (1912) was founded with the express purpose of uniting the best of theatre and the best of film. Belasco's contemporary, Daniel Frohman, joined Adolph Zukor and Edwin S. Porter in the venture. Frohman described the intent in his autobiography: "The idea was to form an alliance between the theatre, its players and its stars, and the screen."[30] In a succession of projects, he signed a number of stage actors to appear in film, including James O'Neill (Eugene O'Neill's father, in *Monte Cristo*); James K. Hackett

(The Prisoner of Zenda); Mrs. Fiske *(Tess of the d'Urbervilles)*; and other players such as John Barrymore and Mary Pickford.

The idea of using popular stage actors in film was not new, dating back to 1903. The practice was recalled by Linda Arvidson, actress and wife of D. W. Griffith:

> As for the Famous Players, long before Adolph Zukor's day, they had been appearing before a movie camera. As far back as 1903 Joseph Jefferson played in his famous "Rip Van Winkle" for the American Mutoscope and Biograph Company. And Sara Bernhardt appeared as *Camille,* in the Eclair Company's two-reel production of the Dumas play in 1911.[31]

Once the idea of the Famous Players was successful and the star system was established, stage actors looked more favorably upon cinema as a profession; high salaries and publicity assured prestige. In addition, some film directors spoke the language of theatre. Individuals such as D. W. Griffith, Sidney Alcott, and J. Searle Dawley had extensive backgrounds on the stage, and sought greater acting realism in film. Griffith was particularly successful at training a new school of actors for the medium. In 1916, he wrote:

> Two years ago there was hardly any real actor depending upon the motion pictures. We paid very little attention to the old stage actors. And at last when we took them and tried them we found they were far beneath in real acting power than the ones we had trained.[32]

Griffith was referring to stage actors trained in the pictorial theatre and oriented to physical display. In contrasting the stage actor with newly-trained film actor, he wrote:

> Somehow, most of the stars who come to us from the regular stage lack sincerity, at least in their earlier efforts before the camera. Mrs. Fiske, in *Tess*, was a notable exception.... Of what use are magnified scenes with only puppet-like actors? Here in America we are training a school of silent actors who bid far to surpass the finest efforts of the Old World Schools.[33]

D. W. Griffith, through his experimentation with inner reality on film, was, in fact, training a whole new group of silent film actors. He emphasized acting subtlety and emotional realism in the stylistic mode of the evolving Stanislavski system.

D. W. Griffith Experiments

The possibility of connecting characterization to behavioral realism was explored by D. W. Griffith, just as it was tested on stage by Stanislavski in Moscow and individual actors on the American stage. Griffith contended that stage actors had to be retrained for the naturalism of the cinema. In 1914, he wrote:

> How many [stage actors] make you believe they are real human beings? No, they "act", that is they use a lot of gestures and make a lot of sounds such as are never seen or heard anywhere else. For range and delicacy, the development of character, the quick transition from one mood to another, I don't know an actress now on the American stage, I don't care how great by reputation, who can begin to touch the work of some of the motion picture actresses. And I'll give you the names if you want them.... Wonderful Mrs. Fiske is, of course, one of the exceptions.[34]

It is noteworthy that Griffith recognized Mrs. Fiske as one of the foremost stage actresses in America and sought a similar approach to the art of acting in film. He insisted his actors speak "clearly and with feeling" even though the film track remained silent.[35] He decried physical exaggeration and sought actors who could "express every single feeling in the entire gamut of emotions" as if it were real life experience.[36] He sought to overcome the obstacle of silence with natural expressiveness:

> The [silent] movie actor cannot add to his art a soft voice; rising or falling inflection; a deep piteous sigh; a quickly intaken breath expressing surprise. There can be no gay, rippling laughter, no solemn tones; no shrieks of fear—not a sound can help the movie actor.[37]

Griffith prided himself on establishing "restraint in expression, raising motion picture acting to the higher plane which has won for it recognition as a genuine art."[38] As his experiments were copied and exploited, film acting further distinguished itself from the stage. Actors were required to respond to the techniques of close-up shooting, repetitive tasks, and building tempos in short scenes. Jacobs aptly noted "movies were now rendered more and more in the film idiom and less and less like a stage play, the emphasis being on delineation of character through detail shots and the selection of incidents."[39]

As characterization demanded more complexity and insight, older actors, such as John Barrymore, were criticized for their outmoded style of performance, with "eyebrow acting," "skyscraper handshakes," "souls of despair," and unnatural "woggle walks."[40] Barrymore simply refused to accept an inner approach to acting: "The better the actor, the more completely is he able to eliminate the personal equation."[41]

That very problem of "personal equation" in acting, dating back to Diderot (1830) and Talma (1877), was temporarily resolved in the twenties, when Stanislavski and the M.A.T. toured America.[42] For the first time, professional actors saw the dramatic impact of a group of actors systematically trained in realism. That system closely paralleled the work that Griffith had been doing in his silent film experiments.

D.W. Griffith, like Stanislavski, attempted to build inner truth through motivated characterizations, the use of emotional recall, and the heightened use of concentration and observation. Such Griffith actresses as Mary

Pickford, Lillian and Dorothy Gish, Laurette Taylor, and Mae Marsh were especially noted for their subdued and realistic performances.[43]

An indication of the similarity of their training and objectives, is revealed by Laurette Taylor's search for psychological and physical truth in approaching her role. Sounding as if she had been trained by Stanislavski, she wrote:

> The most interesting thing to me in acting is the working out of the character, itself, the finding of that which is so uncommon and the small, seemingly insignificant trait which will unconsciously make an appeal to the audience and establish the human appeal.... I want to get right inside the character and act from the heart as well as from the head.[44]

She was reportedly observed by Stanislavski himself, who considered her a brilliant actress.[45] Her work with Griffith marked her as a natural actress, with the ability to convey inner truth and behavioral realism.

Another Griffith actress, Mae Marsh, reportedly worked with the director in establishing inner truth through the use of emotional recall. She recounted an incident in the shooting of *Birth of a Nation* (1915) in which she was supposed to be hiding in the cellar from a frenzied mob attacking the house. Griffith refused to conventionalize the action with "rolling eyes," "dropping to the knees in terror," or "heavy sobbing." He asked her to recall a time in her life when she experienced a similar sensation of fear. The actress recalled that her reaction was "inappropriate"; she responded to the situation with nervous laughter. Griffith tried it immediately, and as Marsh reports, "It was the hysterical laugh of the little girl in the cellar, with the drunken mob raging above, that was, I am sure, far more effective than rolling the eyes or weeping."[46] She recounted a similar incident in the shooting of *Intolerance* (1916) in which her father supposedly died in the big city slums. At first she approached the scene from the standpoint of simple imitation, that is, duplicating another actress's style. After viewing the rushes in the projection room, she knew her performance was not emotionally convincing. D. W. Griffith agreed, and they both sought a technique to heighten the inner reality:

> Mr. Griffith, who was closely studying the action, finally turned in his seat and said: "I don't know what you were thinking about when you did that, but it is evident that it was not about the death of your father."... We began immediately upon the scene again. This time I thought of the death of my own father and the big tragedy to our little home, then in Texas. I could recall the deep sorrow of my mother, my sisters, my brother, and myself.[47]

Here was a classic use of emotional recall, predating the arrival of Stanislavski and the M.A.T. in America by seven years. It was not until the M.A.T. tours in the twenties that American actors first recognized the potential of inner technique for sharpening and unifying their experimentation. Until that time, experimentation with emotional recall was considered erratic and self-indulgent. A popular screen acting text of the period strongly advised against it:

> You cannot portray sorrows which you have yourself experienced; you cannot walk before the camera, goading yourself into simulation of grief by remembering how you felt when you had an ulcerated tooth, or when you couldn't do something you wanted to do, or go somewhere you wanted to go. Your imagination must put you right into the mind of that bereaved [character]. It is *her* grief you must portray, not your own.[48]

Nonetheless, the impetus for emotional realism—or inner truth—was pronounced, and Griffith actors delved seriously into character traits, motivational behavior, and the given environment. Like M.A.T. players, they would study other people in every environment to develop their capacity for observation and identification. Lillian Gish was asked to visit a psychiatric institution to study the inmates and to visit the scene of a bombing to study the victims and their families.[49] Griffith felt this kind of observation was essential for learning about human nature and developing empathy.[50] Stanislavski also advocated observing human nature for building emotional empathy:

> We use not only our past emotions as creative material, but we use feelings that we have had in sympathizing with the emotions of others. . . . so we must study other people, and get as close to them emotionally as we can, until sympathy for them is transformed into feelings of our own.[51]

Griffith's search for a natural style of acting led to a carefully orchestrated rehearsal, with the full use of improvisational technique; much like the practice of the First Studio in Moscow.

> At the initial rehearsal Mr. Griffith would sit on a wooden chair, the actors fanning out in front of him, and, as he called out the plot, they would react, supplying in their own words whatever was appropriate for the scene. . . . By the time that we had run through the story several times, he had viewed the action from every conceivable camera angle. Then he would begin to concentrate on characterization. Often he would run through a scene dozens of times before he achieved the desired effect.[52]

He also used sense-memory technique in rehearsals, similar to the sense-memory exercises derived from Stanislavski's teachings.[53] Lillian Gish recalled: "In rehearsals we were expected to visualize the props—furniture where none stood, windows in blank walls, doors where there was only space. Our physical movements became automatic and our emotions completely involved."[54]

Other contemporary film acting practices featured techniques which Stanislavski later defined and codified, including the "magic If," the analysis of given circumstances, and the use of heightened imagination and concentration.

Stanislavski's "magic If" was used to strengthen imagination and spontaneity, calling upon the actor to envision what he would do *if* he were in the given circumstances of the character. Stanislavski explained: "I call *if* jokingly a 'magic' word because it does much to help an actor get into action."[55] Griffith used a similar technique, supplying the given circumstances and imaginative action through side-coaching technique. A most telling narrative was offered by Lillian Gish, in preparation for her role in *The Mothering Heart*:

> As I rehearsed the scene, Mr. Griffith fed me the reactions of the injured wife: "You feel that you've been humiliated by your husband in public. You think that he doesn't love you any longer because you're carrying his child. You're afraid that he wants to get rid of you." With his intense voice coaching me, I felt the heroine's agony....
>
> After leaving her husband, the wife bears her child alone in a cottage. The infant dies. In her grief she wanders into the garden, picks up a stick, and beats the rose bushes until they are stripped bare. This was Griffith's idea. He was justly famous for the bits of "business" that he injected into his films. Even when they were not really essential to the basic plot, they communicated emotions that he wanted to project. If an actor devised a good piece of business during rehearsals, Mr. Griffith would keep it in.[56]

The "bits of business" which communicated emotions are directly analogous to Stanislavski's later emphasis on the logic of physical actions. The dramatic action is tied directly to the emotional impact of the scene's reality.

Griffith also stressed the importance of analyzing the story and character in preparation for a part. Mae Marsh outlined that technique:

> [In approaching a part] we first look to the plot and theme of the story. We want to know what the author is telling and how he is trying to tell it. We find the big situations and the action that preceded them. More important, we locate the "why" of it.[57]

In essence, she was defining the superobjective of the writer, the given circumstances of the scene, and the motivations of the character.

This kind of experimentation paralleled closely Stanislavski's own work. In *Creating a Role*, he recommended three distinct steps for approaching a character: (1) a period of detailed analysis of the superobjective and the given circumstances of the play, (2) a period of emotional experience involving the creation of inner states of being, the realization of motivations, objectives, and intentions, and (3) a period of physical embodiment involving detailed work on physical actions, facial expression, voice, speech, and movement.

Although Griffith did not know Stanislavski, he experimented with similar training and rehearsal programs. The film director even encouraged his actors to study fencing, dancing, voice, and breath control,[58] as Stanislavski advocated extensive physical and vocal training for the actor. Despite Griffith's creative experiments, the end result was often melodramatic, more than psychologically truthful and emotionally convincing. Griffith actors experimented with inner technique, but their subdued realism was as conventional in its own way as the earlier exaggerated pantomime in films had been. As Vardac observed:

> This "realism" carried restraint to the point where all emotion was expressed by means of a "long, level stare" which might signify keen analytical mind or congenital obtuseness; cold hate or hot passion; warm friendship or sullen enmity; indomitable determination or a touch of hay fever.[59]

He pointed to the development of character types—the villain, the dowager, and so on—and the rise of film melodrama as concomitants of stereotype acting.

One can see the conventionalized realism in any number of Griffith films, beginning with his own acting chores in *Rescued From An Eagle's Nest* (1907) for Edison Studio, through his directorial efforts in *Broken Blossoms* (1919) and *Way Down East* (1920).[60] The melodramatic tone is strong and is evident in the performances of Lillian Gish and Richard Barthelmess. Nonetheless, Griffith actors were generally more aware of the need to underplay their parts, and to approach their roles from the perspective of human nature. Even outside the Griffith stable, certain actors approached their roles from a realistic standpoint. Charlie Chaplin based his characterizations on the realism of human nature[61] and was considered "one of the great actors of all time in any medium" by Lee Strasberg.[62]

One of Griffith's actresses, Lillian Gish, received a letter of commendation from Nemirovich-Danchenko, who cofounded the M.A.T. with Stanislavski:

> I want once more to tell you of my admiration of your genius. In that picture [*The Wind*], the power and expressiveness of your betrayal begat real tragedy. A combination of the greatest sincerity, brilliance and unvarying charm places you in the small circle of the first tragediennes of the world.... It is quite possible that I shall write [of it] again to Russia, where you are the object of great interest and admiration by the people.[63]

Clearly, D. W. Griffith was an important figure in establishing realistic acting standards for American film, just as Belasco popularized realistic detail and understatement in commercial theatre.

The Sound Film Arrives

When *The Jazz Singer* (1929) was released, film acting was thrown into a state of extreme confusion. With the advent of sound, acting for the screen required a new dimension—vocal training. Many silent film stars found their careers at a dead end. One prominent romantic actor, John Gilbert, who had a high-pitched voice, failed to find a job in the talkies. He eventually committed suicide.[64]

Sound films became a lucrative source of revenue for the film studios, and they relied heavily on stage-trained actors in lead roles. However, a classic Pudovkinian problem arose: exaggerated theatrical conventions of the stage were not compatible with the more naturalistic requirements of cinema. Theatrical conventions seemed even less convincing when projected on the screen.

In the early stages of the sound era, technical requirements overshadowed all else. The year 1929 was appropriately deemed "the year of static, photographed stage plays, the year of 'all-talking, all-singing' musicals, the year in which raw sound was exploited in every imaginable way."[65] A number of dramatic plays were translated to screen, but the actor's range of movement was severely limited. Microphones were now in use, and the "noisy" camera was housed in a nonmovable soundproof booth. The result was "canned theatre."[66]

According to one Griffith biographer, the issue of the sound film was discussed at a meeting of the Academy of Motion Picture Arts and Sciences, after the success of *The Jazz Singer*. Griffith reportedly denounced sound as a menace to film art:

> It's a noisy monstrosity. . . It is a chattering horror. It will destroy all we have accomplished in creating a new art. It has no beauty—and beauty is the very basis of pictures. It has no soul. It mouths only gibberish and we should unite against it.[67]

The Academy members applauded loudly, but sound quickly took over the industry, posing problems and adjustments for actors who began their careers in the silent era. Frank Capra, one of the most popular directors of the thirties, recalled some of the problems on the set:

> The biggest trouble we had was from the silent actors who were asked to read lines all of a sudden and memorize lines. And the biggest hangup was the silence. I mean the actual silence [on the set]. The silent actors used to work with people hammering things, and directors shouting at them all the time, and the cameramen yelling. . . And then [with the advent of the microphone] everything was quiet. Suddenly the stillness would settle over [them], and the actors would shake. They weren't used to the silence and this got to them.[68]

Actors moving from the stage to film had unique problems of their own, particularly in the realm of physical restraint and underplaying. Film director George Cukor recalled the problems Laurence Olivier had in transferring his talent from stage to screen in *Wuthering Heights* (1939):

> [Olivier] flung himself here and there. He had done this sort of thing on the stage, and simply didn't know that you had to [underact in films]. Sam Goldwyn and he had a conversation

and then he adjusted his acting, still having the vigor, the flair, but also the reality that is needed for screen acting.[69]

During the sound era, the star system itself changed, and the needs of acting were profoundly affected. Charles Higham summarized that progress:

> In the silent period, the great stars were those who could captivate millions by sheer force of personality, through gift with exaggerated mime, and in their ability to personify certain fixed ideals, ranging from the girl-woman to the Continental charmer, the husky athlete to the glorified lounge lizard.... In the talkie era the very character of acting changed. Broadway became the exemplar and the supplier. [In addition to personality types and stereotypes] there were the actresses and actors who really understood the need for sophistication in their playing, among them Bette Davis, Spencer Tracy, Edward G. Robinson, Humphrey Bogart, and James Cagney.[70]

With the addition of sound, the actor was now much closer to creating the full semblance of reality. The Stanislavski system—which was already introduced to America—served as the most suitable approach to realistic acting for adoption on stage and screen.

3

The System in America: Arrival, Interpretation, Controversy, 1900-1940s

Alla Nazimova Arrives

America's first introduction to the evolving principles of Stanislavski occurred when Alla Nazimova, a student of Stanislavski, toured this country with the St. Petersburg Players from Russia (1905). The touring company apparently modeled their realistic style after the M.A.T.[1] Nazimova's English-speaking debut in *The Chosen People* (1905) was the first definitive example of "the new acting" in America, and was critically acclaimed for its "naturalism," "brilliant interpretation," and "inspired performance."[2] She was signed to a five-year contract by the Shubert's, and often played the heroines in Ibsen plays. *The New York Times* hailed her as "one of the most remarkable actresses of our times"[3]; it ranked her superior to America's own Mrs Fiske.[4] *The New York Dramatic Mirror*, published by Mrs. Fiske's husband, also lauded the unique ability of Nazimova to play two different Ibsen roles so sensitively and realistically.[5] The same artistic quality was noted by *Theatre Magazine*: "That she is able to impersonate two such widely divergent characters [Nora in *A Doll's House;* Hedda in *Hedda Gabler*] with the consummate skill which she has evidenced, speaks wonders for the rare versatility of her polished art."[6]

Nazimova's acting technique reflected the early analytic experimentation of the M.A.T.: "I think not at all of my part, but always of the plot and the central theme and the play of the characters upon each other."[7] She approached her character through a "conscious, technical effort," which she had developed in early experimentation with Stanislavski.[8]

Nazimova's performances were psychologically inspired, a strong contrast to the pictorial realism and declamatory acting typical of the period. For this reason, she was particularly successful with Ibsen plays, and made a considerable impact on the emerging cinema as well. She appeared in more than twenty motion pictures, including such silent film classics as *War Brides* (1916), *Out of the Fog* (1919), *The Brat* (1919), *Heart of a Child* (1920), *Billions* (1920), *Camille* (1921), *A Doll's House* (1922), *Salome,* (1922), *Madonna of the*

Streets (1924), and *My Son* (1925). She continued to work regularly in films throughout the thirties and forties.

Nazimova's work in film marks her as the first authentic link between the early Stanislavski system in Moscow and the silent film era in Hollywood. She reportedly earned over $13,000 a week in the Hollywood of the early twenties,[9] and has been credited with inspiring the same kind of psychological realism in acting that culminated with the momentous tours of the M.A.T.[10]

The Moscow Art Theatre in America

After more than a decade of experimentation, during which Stanislavski refined his system, he brought the M.A.T. to America, opening in New York on 8 January 1923. The production, Tolstoy's *Tsar Fyodor*, featured such players as Stanislavski, Maria Ouspenskaya, Olga Knipper-Chekhova, and Leo and Barbara Bulgakov. The enthusiastic response generated a second tour, which received equally ebullient praise. The drama critic of the *New York Evening Post* wrote that performances were so vivid, it was "almost like an unwarrantable intrusion upon privacy."[11] Similarly, Stark Young, in *Glamour*, marvelled at the M.A.T. players' ability to create "a complete air of human beings living there in the familiar ways of men."[12] Kenneth MacGowan, who assessed the 1923 theatrical season for *Theatre Arts,* specifically commended the M.A.T. for its enlightening contribution to the art of American acting:

> I doubt if any three months of the past three years—perhaps the past thirty—are more crammed with significance for the future of the American theatre than November, December, and January.... Far at the head of this quarter-season, of course, stands the visit of the first theatre of the world: the Moscow Art Theatre. The work of Stanislavski's extraordinary company illuminates all the vital problems that confront the American stage.... It shows us sharply individualized characterizations, a virtuosity of impersonation on the part of each player, the highest proficiency and the most sincere and sustained spiritual effort, and the welding of all the various performers of a play into an ensemble of fluid, varied, yet concerted and pointed quality.[13]

MacGowan asserted that the time has come for this country to learn how to train actors and how to develop a proficient acting technique. Similarly, Ludwig Lewisohn, in *Theatre Magazine* (August 1923), reported that audiences and critics sat "in astonishment and awe ... at the feet of the players from Moscow"; our actors would be capable of achieving the same kind of performance if a given system were available.[14]

Lee Strasberg saw every M.A.T. production and was impressed by the total ensemble effort. He sought the same kind of experience for American actors.[15] Actors in theatre and film were experimenting with the inner approach, but no one could match the unqualified impact and success of the

M.A.T. players. The Stanislavski system provided a cohesive and pragmatic solution to acting goals for stage and film.

Stanislavski commented on the unexpected success of his tour in America:

> We have never had such a success. . . No one seems to have had any idea what our theatre or actors are capable of. . . This should give you an idea at what an embryonic state stage art is [in America] and how eagerly they snatch up everything good that is brought to America.[16]

A special matinee performance was arranged, permitting American actors to see the M.A.T. in practice. John Barrymore, who had been criticized for his "eyebrow acting," said it was "the most amazing performance I have ever had by a million miles in the theatre."[17] The M.A.T. tours provided a vivid impetus and concrete model for achieving a heightened sense of psychological realism in American acting. David Belasco, who had formerly denied the importance of personal involvement in acting, now wrote: "My actors and actresses become letter-perfect in their parts when they forget they are acting and begin actually to live their roles."[18]

The eagerness of American actors to learn the system and to utilize the precepts on stage may have contributed to the desire of several M.A.T. members to emigrate and teach the Stanislavski system in New York. This group included Richard Boleslavski, Maria Ouspenskaya, Leo and Barbara Bulgakov, Tamara Daykarhanova, Vera Soloviova, Andrius Jilinsky, and Michael Chekhov.[19] Each of these individuals not only contributed to the acting styles of the American stage, but appeared in the mainstream of American film in the late thirties and forties, just as Nazimova did in the twenties.

Richard Boleslavski and the American Laboratory Theatre

Richard Boleslavski was perhaps the most influential figure, providing America with its first published look at the principles of the Stanislavski system in April 1923,[20] and teaching the system for the first time in the summer of 1923 at the Neighborhood Playhouse in New York. Boleslavski contended that M.A.T. realism was essentially different from the pictorial realism of the stage spectacle, which America was producing. He asserted that realism did not mean "sordid detail, mechanical cleverness, make-up, nor scenic intricacy. The realism that Stanislavski preaches is internal, not external."[21]

In 1924, Boleslavski opened the American Laboratory Theatre in New York, which he hoped would "push forward the theatrical art of the country twenty years."[22] In fact, the American Laboratory had an inspiring impact on nearly five hundred students during its seven years of activity[23], including Lee Strasberg, Harold Clurman, and Stella Adler.

Boleslavski's *Acting: The First Six Lessons* (1949) consisted of his writings over a ten-year period (1923-1933) and was a seminal influence in defining the Stanislavski system for American actors. As Michael C. Hardy writes:

> Boleslavski's writings and lectures on theatre constitute one of the most important sources of the Stanislavski concepts as they have been understood in the United States. Stanislavski's *An Actor Prepares* was translated into English in 1936, but, until that time, Boleslavski's version of the system was the only systematic treatment available.[24]

The lessons were based on individual components of the early Stanislavski system: "Concentration," "Memory of Emotion," "Dramatic Action," "Characterization," "Observation," and "Rhythm." Boleslavski's account of the system was accurate, but tended to oversimplify the interrelated nature of the system.[25] Moreover, Stanislavski's later theories—particularly the logic of physical actions—remained unknown to Boleslavski.

America's interpretation of the system derives largely from Boleslavski's work. In 1923, he delivered a series of lectures under the title "The Creative Theatre," summarizing the work he intended for the American Laboratory Theatre.[26] It specifically detailed work on concentration and affective memory, which became the springboard for Lee Strasberg's later emphasis. As Hardy noted:

> If a pupil was exposed only to the early work of Boleslavski, his understanding of the system would reflect this emphasis. This was the case with Lee Strasberg, an early student at the Laboratory. His subsequent misplaced emphasis on affective memory radically altered his own version of the system.[27]

In July 1929, Boleslavski published his second lesson in acting, which was concentrated on the affective memory aspect of Stanislavski training. That emphasis—separate from the totality of training—gave undue attention to that one element of the system, which was subsequently exploited by Strasberg in the Group Theatre in 1931. Strasberg recalled his impressions of Boleslavski:

> Boleslavski said in his first talk, "There are two kinds of acting. One believes that the actor can actually experience on the stage. The other believes that the actor only indicates what the character experiences, but does not himself actually experience. The essential thing in such experience is that the actor learns to know and to do, not through mental knowledge, but by *sensory* knowledge." Suddenly I knew "That's it! That's it!" That was the answer I had been searching for.[28]

Strasberg was moved by this one concept, but he "did not stay at the Laboratory long enough to absorb the rest of the system."[29] Affective memory work was eventually complemented by later experimentation with physical action at the American Laboratory Theatre. Both Boleslavski and Ouspenskaya explored this approach, advocating emotional memory "only insofar as it was expressed by action in terms of the play."[30] The sensory work of the American Laboratory Theatre was singled out by Strasberg at the Group Theatre; that concept of inner technique dominated all other aspects of the original Stanislavski system.

The Group Theatre

The Group Theatre was founded in 1931 by Lee Strasberg, Harold Clurman, and Cheryl Crawford with the express purpose of utilizing the Stanislavski system as a basis for training a true ensemble in America. The Group initially stressed the analytic approach to a role, but Stella Adler recalled that this intellectual approach was gradually diminished as the use of actions, improvisations, and affective memory increased.[31]

In the first four years, under Lee Strasberg's direction, the utilization of affective memory and exact emotion became the predominant aspects of the system. Strasberg insisted upon the unraveling of unconscious feelings in the quest for Stanislavskian inner truth. Clurman called him a "fanatic on the subject of emotion. Everything was secondary to it."[32] Strasberg consequently rejected all other acting styles as impractical, including Brecht's, whose dialectical objectivity was in total opposition to emotional subjectivity and inner truth.[33]

The Group Theatre continued to stress analytical and emotional realities until a confrontation occurred between Stella Adler and Lee Strasberg in 1934. Adler met with Stanislavski in Paris, and she expressed her disillusionment with the system. He offered to help her understand his method through work, demonstration, and explanation.[34] They worked in daily sessions, about five hours a day, for over a month.[35] When Adler returned to the Group Theatre in New York, she proceeded to demonstrate the system as taught by Stanislavski—which was at variance with Strasberg's interpretation. Adler's demonstration gave new stress to actions, to the circumstances of the play, and the imagination of the actor, rather than the personal feelings of the actor.[36] The Group felt that Strasberg had misled them with undue emphasis on affective memory. Harold Clurman recounted the impact of Adler's return:

> To put it bluntly, she had discovered that our use of the Stanislavski system had been incorrect. An undue emphasis on the "exercises" of affective memory had warped our work with the actor. Strasberg's first reaction to this declaration was the charge that Stanislavski had gone back on himself. Later, however, he decided to take advantage of the suggestions furnished by Stella's report, and to use what he could of the "innovations" in Stanislavski's method.[37]

A positive response to Adler and a critical response to Strasberg was the prevalent attitude. Group member Robert Lewis recalled:

> Stella's report was a breath of fresh air. It was right from the horse's mouth. Until that time Strasberg was considered a disciple of Stanislavski. To the Group, he was now excommunicated. All that he had been doing was digging, probing, "kvetching." We were all

very excited—for this was more the theatre! It was a turning point, which eventually brought about the departure of Strasberg from the Group. The spell had been broken.[38]

Another group member, Sanford Meisner, had a similar reaction, which capsulized the theoretical differences up to that point in the Group's approach to acting:

> More important than our apparent misuse of emotional memory was the fact that we were using circumstances from our own lives. What Stella told us was that Stanislavski concentrated on the circumstances of the play—or the background of the situation in the play. Until then the Group had always worked from sense memory but never from given circumstances.[39]

Stanislavski had his own recollections of his meeting with Stella Adler, whom he remembered as "a completely panic stricken woman." He offered to work with her "only to restore the reputation of my system. I wasted a whole month on it. It turned out that everything she had learnt was right."[40] She already had a firm grounding in the system through training with Boleslavski and Ouspenskaya. Stanislavski worked with her on "throughline of action" and "task," which he considered the "crux of the whole system." In that regard, Adler was correct in reporting that the system's proper emphasis was on the given circumstances of the script, and logical action for the character.[41]

Strasberg maintained that Adler misrepresented the Group's activities, and that the Group did incorporate given circumstances and physical action into their exercises. Still, he acknowledged that the Group was fundamentally concerned with inner reality, "the particular characteristic of our work which excited people."[42] He viewed himself as inspired by Stanislavski's ideas, but curiously avoided contact with Stanislavski throughout his life. Strasberg toured Moscow in 1934, observed the M.A.T., met with Meyerhold, and studiously avoided any contact with Stanislavski. Strasberg eventually claimed he was angered by a weak performance at the M.A.T., and was afraid he would embarrass Stanislavski with his criticism. It was not until the 1970s that Strasberg would look back at the incident as a "lost opportunity" to learn more about Stanislavski's ideas.[43]

Although Strasberg was criticised for modifying the system according to his own interpretation, his stress on emotional reality was relevant and effective for dealing with realistic plays and films. Throughout the twenties and thirties, a number of outstanding American dramatists created major works for the stage. Both realistic and stylistic efforts appeared in the works of Eugene O'Neill, Clifford Odets, Lillian Hellman, S.N. Behrman, Marc Connelly, Thornton Wilder, Elmer Rice, Maxwell Anderson, Robert Sherwood, and Sidney Kingsley. Many of the plays were well suited to the acting style of the modified Stanislavski system, with artistic stress on emotional truth and psychological reality. That same stress fit the evolving requirements of film, where more naturalistic characters and conflicts were developing.

4

The System Comes to Hollywood:
Crossovers into Film, 1930-1950s

Stanislavski's Protégés in Hollywood

While the Group Theatre was active in New York, a more naturalistic style of acting developed in Hollywood. The cynicism of the Depression was reflected in films such as *Little Caesar* (1930), *Public Enemy* (1931), and *Quick Millions* (1931). As Arthur Knight observed, there was

> a realism of character and incident about these films that was in sharp contrast to the talky problem plays that surrounded them. They had action, racy dialogue, the sharply naturalistic performances of people like James Cagney, Edward G. Robinson, Joan Blondell, Lee Tracy, Paul Muni, and George Bancroft.[1]

Many film actors of the thirties and forties seemed particularly responsive to the use of emotional memory techniques, which dominated the Group Theatre approach to acting. Spencer Tracy recalled personal situations and feelings which might be transferred to the film character he portrayed;[2] Margaret O'Brian used powerful personal imagery to build hysterical scenes in her films;[3] Paul Muni used direct appeal to the emotions as well as personal substitutions and associations:

> I often note ... associations and parallel feelings which have come to me.... When I read a scene which has never even remotely touched my life, I use the associative method or substitution, thinking of situations which may have nothing in common with the one I am about to play, but which, for me, will evoke the mood and feeling of my scene.[4]

The use of similar techniques in film and theatre may represent coincidental experimentation—as in Griffith's time—but more likely is indicative of the significant crossover of Stanislavski talent from stage to screen. The thirties and forties were marked by that growing trend.

Richard Boleslavski, for example, left the American Laboratory Theatre in 1929 and moved to Hollywood, where he directed sixteen films in the next seven years. These included *Rasputin and the Empress* (1932), *Les Miserables* (1935), which was nominated for Best Picture in the Academy Awards, *Theodora Goes Wild* (1936), *The Garden of Allah* (1936), and *The Last of Mrs. Cheney* (1937). Like other stage directors of the period, Boleslavski sought to use his skills with actors on screen:

> At this time, with the advent of sound in the motion picture industry, Hollywood was paying high prices to acquire stage directors who presumably would be able to handle the new dialogue aspects in films. Boleslavski was one of many theatre professionals who were drawn to Hollywood by lucrative salaries.[5]

At first, despite some initial directorial efforts, Boleslavski could not establish himself in Hollywood. He was reportedly fired from three film jobs in a row.[6] He was frustrated in his attempt to find work, and was ready to leave the West Coast:

> He was three years on the Coast before anyone would give him any sort of chance. Just before he got his "break" with *Rasputin* [1932] he wrote me that he was going to give up— that pictures evidently were not for him.[7]

Boleslavski decided to remain in Hollywood, where he completed the third, fourth, fifth, and sixth lessons in acting for *Theatre Arts Monthly* (1931-1932). His third lesson specifically addressed the problems of motion picture acting, and showed how the Stanislavski concept of dramatic action helps prepare an actor for the irregular nature of film work.

As a film director, Boleslavski relied heavily on the use of the Stanislavski system. He used the precepts of dramatic action and script analysis in all his directorial efforts. Hardy, who conducted extensive research on Boleslavski, maintains that "the consistency of his productions resulted from his predominant concern with defining and elaborating the 'spine of the play.'"[8] Francis Fergusson, who worked with Boleslavski and Ouspenskaya at the American Laboratory Theatre, concurred: "Boleslavski, when working on a play, would always devote the first couple of weeks to 'finding the action;' the main action, or 'spine' of each character, and the changes of that action in each situation of the play.[9]

Boleslavski's ability to work with producers and actors became a vital asset. He developed a reputation for unusual calm, artistry, and reliability, eventually directing a variety of films, including the critically acclaimed *Les Miserables* (1935) with Frederick March and Charles Laughton. It focused on human relationships, and was highly praised for its dramatic brilliance and mood. The Motion Picture Academy nominated it as Best Picture of the year; the *New York Times* nominated it as one of the ten best films of 1935. Utilizing the precepts of the Stanislavski system, he concentrated on the analysis of script, character, and action, as well as the technique of improvisation. He worked improvisational techniques into rehearsals for *Theodora Goes Wild* (1936) with Irene Dunne and Melvyn Douglas. The result was a spontaneity in performance that was quite different in style from his earlier works.[10]

A thorough and detailed analysis of Boleslavski's directorial style in film concluded:

> The main objective which Boleslavski accomplished with his actors was to keep their attention riveted on the acting problem of the moment. His actors stray very little in terms of their focus, and it is their intensity that is remarkable rather than any alterations in their "star" images.[11]

He undoubtedly influenced the actors he directed, including many acclaimed film performers of the period, Joan Crawford, William Powell, Robert Montgomery, Lionel Barrymore, Ethel Barrymore, and John Barrymore.

Critics generally agreed that Boleslavski achieved the highest sense of realism from his actors. One reviewer acclaimed the Boleslavski actor who "plays with restraint, and thanks to direction, gives the most persuasively human and least theatric performance."[12] Another reviewer praised the "subtle sense of dramatic values and carefully restrained delivery that brings the character genuinely to life."[13] A number of different film reviewers agreed: Boleslavski's screen characters were created in the naturalistic mode of life.[14]

Boleslavski successfully adapted the Stanislavskian precepts of realistic acting to the requirements of film, and proved the practicality and flexibility of the system. In this sense, he may be considered a primary link between the Stanislavski system as practiced in Moscow and the developing style of screen realism in Hollywood in the thirties.

Boleslavski's colleague at the American Laboratory Theatre, Maria Ouspenskaya, also made the transition into film. Like Boleslavski, she was one of the original members of the First Studio in Moscow, and studied with Stanislavski and Sulerzhitski at the Moscow Art Theatre. She moved to Hollywood in 1936 for a role in Sydney Howard's adaption of *Dodsworth* (1936), which was hailed as "brilliantly acted, thoroughly absorbing."[15] Ouspenskaya was singled out for "contributing an outstanding characterization as the Baroness Von Obersdorf."[16] She stayed in Hollywood, working in twenty motion pictures including such diverse projects as *King's Row* (1941), *Frankenstein Meets the Wolf Man* (1943), *Tarzan and the Amazons* (1945), and *I've Always Loved You* (1946). She opened an acting school on the West Coast in 1939, where she taught Hollywood actors the principles of the Stanislavski system, to which she remained dedicated.[17]

Boleslavski and Ouspenskaya were not the only former M.A.T. members to move permanently to Hollywood. Alla Nazimova was at that time already established as a leading actress and continued to star in films such as *Zaza* (1939), *Blood and Sand* (1941), and *The Bridge of San Luis Rey* (1944). Leo Bulgakov, who opened an acting school in 1939, directed two features, *I'll*

Always Love You (1935) and *Marusia* (1938), and performed in four films, including *For Whom the Bell Tolls,* which was nominated for Best Picture of 1943 by the Motion Picture Academy. Similarly, Michael Chekhov moved to Hollywood where he opened his acting studio in 1939 and appeared in ten major features, including *Song of Russia* (1944), *Spellbound* (1945), which was nominated for Best Picture, and *Specter of the Rose* (1946).

These first generation students of Stanislavski brought the system directly to the screen, expanding its use throughout the thirties and forties in Hollywood.

The Second Generation in Film

The "second generation" of actors trained in the Stanislavski system— primarily the Group Theatre in New York—were at first reluctant to become involved with the motion picture medium. Hollywood, as Harold Clurman writes, was the symbol of "crass commercialism," rather than an artistic form for dramatic expression:

> In the Group in those days, Hollywood was the symbol in the show world of money-making unrelated to any other ideal. It was so remote to us then that we hardly took pains to scorn it. We saw movies occasionally, and liked them, perhaps, but we rarely thought of how or where they were made or that we or any of our kind might be connected with their making.[18]

Elia Kazan had similar recollections, even after certain group members made the transition to film: "A lot of Group Theatre people like John Garfield, Franchot Tone, [J.Edward] Bromberg, left for Hollywood. We looked down on them, we thought it was a defect of idealism on their part, they were traitors."[19]

Despite the Group's elitist attitude toward Hollywood, many of their members entered the mainstream of film and they were considered a primary resource for Hollywood talent. In 1936, Jack Wildberg attempted to sign them all to a film contract; Elia Kazan signed on for two hundred dollars a week.[20] Kazan worked as a film director in the thirties and early forties, then directed some of the major motion pictures of the decade. Among his many films were the period classics, *A Tree Grows in Brooklyn* (1945), *Gentleman's Agreement* (1948), *Panic in the Streets* (1950), *A Streetcar Named Desire* (1951), *Viva Zapata* (1952), *On the Waterfront* (1954). *East of Eden* (1955), *Baby Doll* (1956), *A Face in the Crowd* (1957), *Splendor in the Grass* (1961), and *America, America* (1963). Kazan continued his directorial efforts throughout the seventies and eighties, using the precepts of the Stanislavski system in each of his films (Kazan's use of the system is discussed in Chapter 6).

Other Group members who entered film in the thirties and forties included Stella Adler, who made her film debut in *Love on Toast* (1938) under the pseudonym "Stella Ardler."[21] Harold Clurman was an associate producer for Columbia Pictures in 1941 and directed *Deadline at Dawn* (1945) for R.K.O. (written by Group member Clifford Odets).[22] Lee Strasberg moved to Hollywood in 1944, and spent three years directing screen tests for 20th Century Fox Studios. He was unable to advance his screen career, and returned to New York in frustration. After a career of training other actors, Strasberg finally achieved his belated screen debut in *Godfather II* (1975), seven years before his death. For that performance, he was nominated for an Academy Award.[23] Strasberg later appeared in *Going in Style* (1979), and *Boardwalk* (1979).

As the Group Theatre members joined the growing ranks of Stanislavski-trained actors in film, the system gained marked recognition, exposure, and prominence. It was not until the late forties and fifties, however, with the advent of the Actor's Studio (1947) that America's modified approach to the system dominated the Hollywood acting style. The Actor's Studio provided a common ground for professional stage and film training, with particular emphasis on developing and controlling emotional and analytical processes. This modified approach to Stanislavski was totally congruent with the plays of William Inge, Arthur Miller, and Tennessee Williams, as well as the thematic development of films, which were now largely keyed to inner psychological conflicts.[24] The Actor's Studio and its Method uniquely complemented the emerging needs of cinema in the fifties and sixties.

1. *Constantin Stanislavski,* from a performance in "The Cherry Orchard."
(Courtesy of Billy Rose Theatre Collection, The New York Public Library at
Lincoln Center/Astor, Lenox and Tilden Foundations)

2. *Constantin Stanislavski*. Publicity portrait from the Moscow Art Theatre Tours. (Courtesy of Billy Rose Theatre Collection, The New York Public Library at Lincoln Center/Astor, Lenox and Tilden Foundations)

3. *Alla Nazimova.* Publicity still from *Salome* (1922). Nazimova was the first authentic link between Stanislavski and the early silent films in Hollywood. (Courtesy of Museum of Modern Art/Film Stills Archive)

4. *Richard Boleslavski.* Boleslavski was one of the most influential figures in defining Stanislavski's ideas for American actors. He opened the American Lab Theatre in 1924 and moved to Hollywood in 1929, where he directed several major films. (Courtesy of Billy Rose Theatre Collection, The New York Public Library at Lincoln Center/Astor, Lenox and Tilden Foundations)

5. Richard Boleslavski directed Lionel Barrymore and Ethel Barrymore in M.G.M.'s *Rasputin and the Empress* (1933). (Courtesy of Museum of Modern Art/Film Stills Archives)

6. Boleslavski directed Irene Dunne and Melvyn Douglas in the Columbia Pictures show *Theodora Goes Wild* (1936). (Courtesy of Museum of Modern Art/Film Stills Archives)

7. *Maria Ouspenskaya.* Publicity still from the film *Mystery of Marie Roget* (1942). Ouspenskaya, like Boleslavski, was one of the original members of the Moscow Art Theatre. She was a partner in the American Lab Theatre (1924), and moved to Hollywood in the early 1930s, where she was featured in many films of the period. (Courtesy of Billy Rose Theatre Collection, The New York Public Library at Lincoln Center/Astor, Lenox and Tilden Foundations)

8. *David Wark Griffith.* D.W. Griffith prided himself on raising motion picture acting to a genuine art. As a film director, he attempted to build inner truth through motivated characterizations. (Courtesy of Museum of Modern Art/Film Stills Archives)

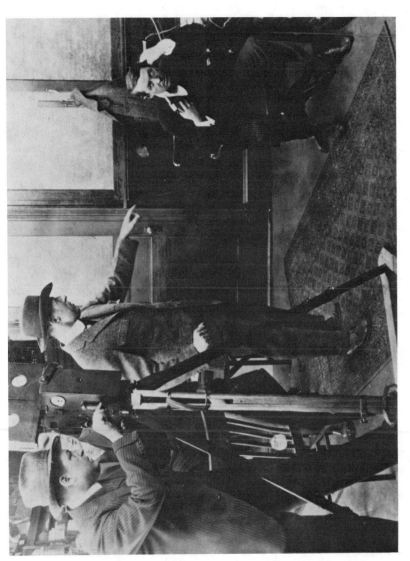

9. D. W. Griffith directs Henry B. Walthall, as cameraman Billy Bitzer films the action. Griffith sought a natural style of acting on film, and experimented with artistic techniques in a rehearsal and production. (Courtesy of Museum of Modern Art/Film Stills Archives)

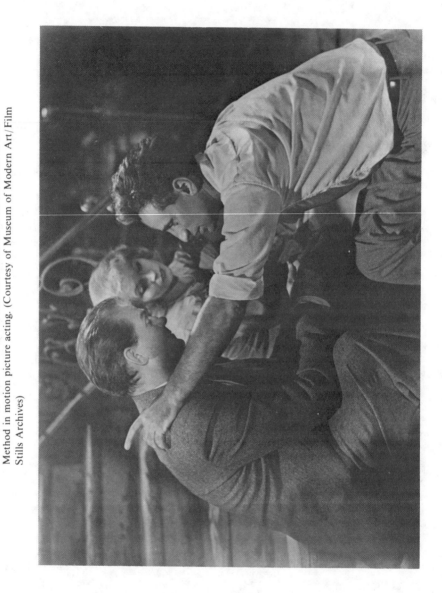

10. Elia Kazan directed Karl Malden and Vivien Leigh in *A Streetcar Named Desire* (1951). This film focused new attention on the effectiveness of The Method in motion picture acting. (Courtesy of Museum of Modern Art/Film Stills Archives)

11. *Elia Kazan.* Former member of the Group Theatre, Kazan founded The Actors Studio in 1947 with Robert Lewis and Cheryl Crawford. He had a significant impact on the use of The Method in American motion pictures. (Courtesy of Museum of Modern Art/Film Stills Archives)

12. Kazan directed Rod Steiger and Marlon Brando in *On the Waterfront* (1954). The film won multiple acting and directing awards in the Motion Picture Academy competition for that year. (Courtesy of Museum of Modern Art/Film Stills Archives)

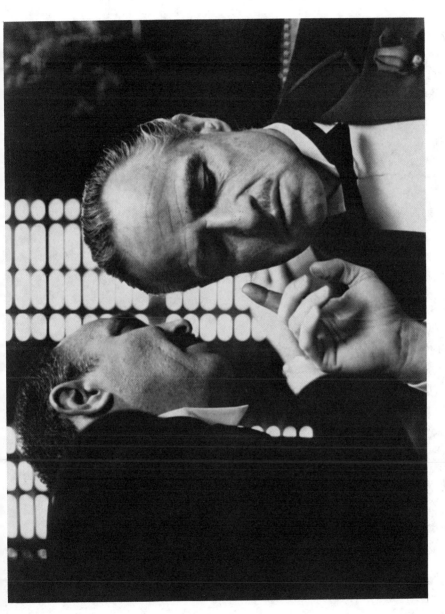

13. Marlon Brando in *The Godfather* (1972). Brando was a member of the Actors Studio since its founding in 1947. (Courtesy of Museum of Modern Art/Film Stills Archives)

14. Al Pacino in *The Godfather* (1972). Pacino joined the Actors Studio in 1966, and became co-Artistic Director with Ellen Burstyn. (Courtesy of Museum of Modern Art/Film Still Archives)

15. Lee Strasberg, surrounded by George Burns and Art Carney, in *Going in Style* (1979). Strasberg was the major proponent of The Method, and was the controversial Artistic Director of the Actors Studio until his death in 1982. (Courtesy of Museum of Modern Art/Film Stills Archives)

16. Dustin Hoffman in *Kramer vs. Kramer* (1979). Hoffman played a wide range of film roles stressing the versatility of character. He joined the Actors Studio in 1966. (Courtesy of Museum of Modern Art/Film Still Archives)

17. Paul Newman starred in *The Verdict* (1982). Newman joined the Actors
     Studio at its inception in 1947. He became President of the Studio in
     the 1980s. (Courtesy of Museum of Modern Art/Film Stills Archives)

The Method and the Actors Studio: Experiments and Impact, 1940-1970s

The Method and the Actors Studio

The Actors Studio was founded in New York in 1947 by three former members of the Group Theatre who wanted to carry on the Group Theatre tradition: Elia Kazan, Robert Lewis, and Cheryl Crawford. The studio was small, dedicated to the principle of providing a place for actors to work. Kazan recalls:

> There wasn't much to it, just two classes; I taught one and Bob Lewis the other.... I took the basic exercises of the Stanislavski method—developing the senses, developing imagination, developing spontaneity, developing the force of the actor, and above all, arousing his emotional resources. I had taken those classes myself from Clurman and Strasberg in my time.[1]

From the outset, the Stanislavskian principles of the Actors Studio attracted motion picture actors as well as theatre actors. Some of the students in Lewis's first class included Montgomery Clift, Marlon Brando, Eli Wallach, Karl Malden, Mildred Dunnock, John Forsythe, and Maureen Stapleton, many of whom were active figures in both film and stage.[2]

In 1948, Robert Lewis left the studio, and Kazan needed a replacement. After a few guest teachers, Lee Strasberg was invited to join, and in 1951, he was appointed artistic director. Kazan implied the choice was deliberate and ideal,[3] but Robert Lewis remembered it quite differently:

> Kazan opposed Strasberg right from the beginning. When they had to bring in a teacher they tried [Sanford] Meisner, [Josh] Logan—anybody but Strasberg. But Gadge [Kazan] always accommodated himself and got Lee to teach—beginning with history of the theatre. Gadge thought a lot of Lee's techniques were strange and he always complained to me. But once Lee got in at the Studio an attempt was made to put him on the map.[4]

Lewis felt that Strasberg would only denigrate the potential of the Actors Studio, particularly through his excessive use of emotional and analytical probing:

The Adler affair proved that Strasberg was mistaken. And now that the Actors Studio has re-impowered him he had found a whole new generation and is doing the same thing—making the same mistakes over again.[5]

Similarly, Kevin McCarthy, a founding member of the Actors Studio, claimed that Kazan wanted to keep Strasberg out of the Studio at all costs.[6]

Nonetheless, Strasberg took over, and the Studio developed an aura of self-indulgence and analytical mystique. As in the Group Theatre, he continued his stress on analytic probing of the unconscious and the use of strong personal experiences. The physical side of the Stanislavski system was virtually discarded in this modification, now known as The Method.[7]

The table on page 53 summarizes the difference between the original system and the Method. It can be seen that Stanislavski stressed imagination as the core of acting, and sought emotional truth from the text of the play. Strasberg sought emotional truth from the unconscious of the actor. This approach, which was highly controversial, had particular appeal and power in cinema, where close-up acting underscored the intimacy of a scene.

Stanislavski's original emphasis on inner technique and intellectual technique (script analysis) was incorporated into the Method but the physicality of the system was totally dismissed, and replaced by analytical considerations. According to Strasberg, the actor must be free of inhibitions in order to achieve emotional truthfulness.[8] The same emotional truthfulness was achieved by Stanislavski through the justified and motivated "logic of physical actions," which was never explored by Strasberg.

Strasberg was a defender of typecasting, maintaining that it maximized awareness of the character and eased the merger process of self with character:

The simplest examples of Stanislavski's ideas are actors such as Gary Cooper, John Wayne, and Spencer Tracy. They try not to act but to be themselves, to respond or react. They refuse to do or say anything they feel not to be consonant with their own characters.[9]

In fact, Stanislavski did not condone typecasting, claiming it limited the creative potential and versatility of the actor. In an undated article, "Types of Actors," he suggested, "Isn't it natural that roles externally handed down will be played in an externally fixed manner?"[10] Nonetheless, the typecasting theory is virtually mandated by the requirements of film, where it enhances the credibility and realism of the character on screen.

Lee Strasberg's interpretation of Stanislavski was heavily criticized by those who adhered closer to the original Russian principles. The resulting conflicts centered around the Studio's approach to inner technique, that is, the use and importance of affective memory, the probing into the unconscious life of the actor, the conceptual merger of self with role ("living the role").

The Stanislavski System Compared to The Method

	Stanislavski System	The Method
The Core Experience of Acting	Imagination: derived from the given circumstances of the play.	Emotions; derived from personal experiences and subconscious of the actor.
Developmental Techniques for Training the Actor	(1) Intellectual (script and role analysis). (2) Inner (emotional recall, imagination, observation, concentration, sensory awareness). (3) External (physical expression, body, voice, and movement). (Later: "logic of physical actions" replaces emphasis on inner technique).	(1) Intellectual (script and role analysis). (2) Inner (emotional recall, imagination, observation, concentration, sensory awareness). (3) Psychoanalytical (using unconscious feelings and experiences). (Inner technique remains dominant, with addition of analytic probing).
Goal of Training	Truth on stage through organic unity of inner and outer spheres during performance.	Inner truth through psychological freedom; breaking inhibitions offstage and on.
Predisposition Toward Analytic Probing of the Actor's Personal Experiences	Not necessary for dramatic action in a play.	Vital for awakening consciousness and awareness in the actor.
Predisposition Toward Type-Casting	Limits the versatility of the actor.	Maximizes consonance of self with character.
On "Merging" With the Character	The logic of physical actions (i.e., justified actions) will lead to merger during performance; must sustain through performance with awareness of reality.	Personality identification will lead to merger; must sustain throughout role preparation and performance to maximize character portrayal.

It might be helpful to contrast the prevailing attitudes among leading advocates of the Stanislavski system, with the Method principles of Strasberg. Unlike all other proponents of the Stanislavski system today, Strasberg maintained that affective memory was the "central experience" in acting.[11] Like Eugene Vakhtangov, he defined affective memory as the recall of unconscious emotional experience, which the actor can evoke at will.[12] It has already been shown that Stanislavski relied primarily upon the imagination of the actor. In "The Art of the Actor and Director," written for the *Encyclopaedia Britannica* in the late twenties, Stanislavski wrote: "[M]y artistic training of an actor . . . uses the means of imagination to reach the affective (emotion) memory."[13]

Other contemporary followers of Stanislavski held similar theories and viewpoints. Stella Adler discouraged the use of affective memory except as a frame of reference for the given action of the play. Like Stanislavski, she stressed imagination as the core experience in acting:

> To go back to a feeling of emotion of one's own experience I believe to be unhealthy. It tends to separate you from the play, from the action of the play, from the circumstances of the play, and from the author's intention.[14]

Similarly, one of the founding members of the First Studio in Moscow, Vera Soloviova, did not feel that emotional recall was always essential: "Stanislavski used to say, 'If the part comes to you spontaneously, you don't have to go through affective memory.'"[15] Sanford Meisner, a Group Theatre member who became head of acting at the Neighborhood Playhouse, shared the original stress on imagination as the key to spontaneity. Instead of probing the unconscious, he advocated an imaginative "fantasy" which could be developed and controlled by the actor.[16]

The Actors Studio was highly criticized for delving into the individual psyche of the actor, particularly in "private moment" exercises.[17] The "private moment" calls upon the actor to recreate intimate situations, thoughts, and actions with fellow actors. Strasberg defended the exercise on the grounds that it strengthens concentration and fights emotional and physical blocks:

> If the actor can recreate these moments of private concentration, they might strengthen his concentration to such an extent, that he can do things on stage which are difficult to do even in life. Also, privacy could be developed to such an extent, that he can behave on stage, in a way he can not even behave in life.[18]

The notion was based on Stanislavski's idea of the actor's being private in public, but was extended to include intimate moments of concentration and action. Strasberg wanted to free the actor's inhibitions and considered this the distinguishing factor between his own work and Stanislavski's.[19]

In defiance of the Method's analytic approach, Sanford Meisner wrote:

> It is not in the province of the acting teacher nor in his capabilities to attempt to penetrate into the hidden, untamperable regions of the actor's personality. . . . I have had even more extensive experience with dentists than with psychoanalysts but that doesn't license me to pull a tooth. Of course, out of my dental experience I do recognize a puffy jaw may dictate a certain type of medical attention, but I do not feel inclined to take the work upon myself. I humbly offer this as a precept.[20]

Similarly, Robert Lewis accused Strasberg of usurping a psychoanalyst's role, and a psychoanalyst cautioned against triggering a latent illness in neurotic actors.[21] Harold Clurman referred to Strasberg's analytic approach as "therapy, not artistry"[22] and argued that the Method approach leads to a private cult that "becomes a distortion of art in general and of Stanislavski's teachings in particular."[23]

As a matter of record, Stanislavski himself did not advocate introspection and private behavioral analysis. As Boleslavski observed:

> Although in Stanislavski's technique, much emphasis is placed upon the inner spirit, the emotions, and the soul, he would be the last man to infer that the theatre should be made a laboratory for the exclusive study of inspection. It is dramatic action that makes the theatre alive.[24]

It was not until the mid-sixties that the psychoanalytic approach to acting was finally re-examined in light of Stanislavski's later ideas. To help correct the American misinterpretation, members of the M.A.T. held a series of seminars in New York (1964), where they responded to questions about the emotional and physical context of the Stanislavski system.[25] The Russian actors emphasized the fact that Stanislavski abandoned affective memory exercises long before his death in 1938, and considered the method of physical actions the highlight of his work in later years.

Another major influence in disseminating the later teachings of Stanislavski was Sonia Moore, who studied at the Third Studio of the M.A.T. As an actress and teacher in America, she has attempted to correct this country's misunderstanding of the system, largely through her writings and the American Center for Stanislavski Theatre Art, which she founded in New York. She has maintained that the true system is the one Stanislavski developed in his later life, that is, the *unification* of inner and outer techniques.

In contrast, Strasberg maintained his emphasis on affective memory and the importance of psychoanalytic probing.[26] The Actors Studio, the stepchild of Strasberg, has kept alive that singularly American interpretation of the early Stanislavski system.

Experiments in Production

The history of the Actors Studio is marked by various attempts to create and produce dramatic works for the stage and screen. The actors, writers, and directors associated with the Studio regularly experimented in workshop situations, and wanted to bring the creative results to the public.

One of the earliest and most successful experiments was in cable television. In 1948, under the direction of Elia Kazan and Cheryl Crawford, the Studio produced fifty-six dramatic programs based largely on short stories and one-act plays. The series featured Studio actors, directors, and stage managers. The first program, *Portrait of Madonna* (September, 1948) was written by Tennessee Williams, and starred Jessica Tandy, who received outstanding reviews for her Blanche Dubois-like characterization. The second program, *Night Club* (October, 1948) won critical acclaim, and starred Maureen Stapleton, Cloris Leachman, and Lee Grant.

The series continued to present strong plays and powerful performances, garnering very positive reviews. In its first season on ABC, the Actors Studio won a Peabody Award for its contribution to television drama. The citation reads:

> To the Actors Studio for its uninhibited and brilliant pioneering in the field of televised drama.... In the opinion of the judges, the Actors Studio is the first to recognize that drama on television is neither a stage play nor a movie, but a separate and distinct new art form.[27]

The series was picked up by CBS in the second season, and the reviews remained impressive. However, the series came to a halt in 1950. Various attempts were made to revive the series over the years, but those attempts never met with success.

In those early years, a number of important Method-trained actors were first introduced to television, including Martin Balsam, Richard Boone, Mildred Dunnock, Tom Ewell, Lee Grant, Julie Harris, Kim Hunter, Cloris Leachman, E.G. Marshall, Kevin McCarthy, Nehemiah Persoff, William Redfield, Eva Marie Saint, Maureen Stapleton, Jo Van Fleet, Eli Wallach, and David Wayne.

Throughout the next decade, the Actors Studio did not have a television series or a legitimate theatre of its own. Individual actors, writers, and directors pressured Strasberg and Kazan to help develop a Studio Theatre, but Strasberg thought it would be inappropriate for the experimental nature of the Studio. Moreover, he thought a space for the Actors Studio should be as illustrious as its namesake; no such theatre was available.

When Kazan left the Studio to become director of the Lincoln Center for the Performing Arts, the Actors Studio was thought likely to become the nation's repertory theatre. However, politics and other conflicts intervened, and the Studio was left without a home for production. Consequently, in 1962, the Actors Studio announced the formation of its own Actors Studio Theatre. Along with the well wishes of the theatrical establishment, the Actors Studio received telegrams of support and congratulations from Hollywood members of the Studio, among them Joanne Woodward, Jennifer Jones, Paul Newman, Tony Franciosa, Marilyn Monroe, Jane Fonda, George Peppard, Maureen Stapleton, Clifford Odets, Eva Marie Saint, Jeff Hayden, Carroll Baker, and Jack Garfein.[28]

As it turned out, the Actors Studio Theatre was destined to meet with a series of failures, largely due to the artistic compromises, administrative weaknesses, and erratic policies of artistic director Lee Strasberg.[29] After repetitive problems in repertory, casting, and directing, the Actors Studio Theatre was invited to present its work to the World Theatre Festival in London (1965). Strasberg selected *Three Sisters* and *Blues for Mr. Charlie* to represent the Studio. Both plays were unmitigated disasters due to last minute cast substitutions, artisitic conflicts, and questionable administrative judgments.

In London, *Blues for Mr. Charlie* was severely criticized for its "uniformly bad acting"; *Three Sisters* was considered "absurd and agonizing" to watch, "incredibly self-indulgent" in performance. The cast included George C. Scott, Kim Stanley, Sandy Dennis and Nan Martin. Lee Strasberg, who directed the play, blamed the entire cast for the debacle. The actors bitterly refuted the charge:

> George C. Scott stood up and, barely controlling his own rage, said threateningly, "Mr. Strasberg, you called us together here to tell us the papers were right? That we're lousy actors? Do you mean to blame the actors for last night's fiasco!" Several of the actors feared for the artistic director's safety. Strasberg quickly turned around and walked out.[30]

The Actors Studio ended with that final performance in London.

While the Actors Studio floundered in indecision and erratic productions, the Ely Landau Company announced a joint venture with the company in 1964 to produce twelve theatre productions on videotape and film. The first project was *Three Sisters* with Shelley Winters and Sandy Dennis. The film was released theatrically more than a decade after the venture began; the brief test run met with extremely harsh reviews.[31]

After the debacle of the London performances, the Actors Studio tried to revamp its organization, but never fully overcame the creative and administrative problems posed by its artistic director. In the late sixties, Strasberg began a number of efforts to bolster the image of the Actors Studio, initiating a forum for invited lecturers, reviving the playwrights and directors unit (which was long dormant), and creating a separate entity, the Lee Strasberg Theatre Institutes in New York and Los Angeles. The institutes were designed to provide intensive training in Method acting techniques.

Strasberg was a controversial figure during his reign at the Actors Studio. On the one hand he was seen as an administrative stumbling block, yet he was also the creative impetus for artistic experimentation. His Method technique had a significant impact on theatre and film acting in this country and abroad.

6

The Method as Mainstream: Theatre and Film Acting, 1950-1970s

American Theatre in the Fifties and Sixties

The Actors Studio and the Method fit comfortably into the theatrical milieu of the fifties. Psychological themes and characters dominated the mainstream of realistic drama, and the Method approach to acting was totally congruent with the naturalistic plays. As Brockett and Findlay noted:

> The dominant style in the American theatre from the late 1940s until about 1960 was a theatricalized realism comprised of acting which emphasized intense psychological truth and of visual elements which eliminated nonessentials but retained realistic outlines. It combined near-naturalism in performance with stylization in settings. This mode was popularized by the director Elia Kazan and the designer Jo Mielziner through such productions as *A Streetcar Named Desire* (1947) and *Death of a Salesman* (1949).[1]

Elia Kazan's directorial work was marked by extensive use of the Method. His production of *A Streetcar Named Desire* represented the complete absorption of the Method into the mainstream of theatre and film. The theatrical production was staged in 1947; Brooks Atkinson evaluated the play in these terms:

> Elia Kazan's direction was sensitive and scrupulous, and the confrontations and the climaxes were overwhelming. The tenderness and the brutality were woven into a single strand of panic and doom. Marlon Brando became a star on the basis of the sullen, brutish brother-in-law he played vividly; and Karl Malden's portrait of the homely drudge named Mitch began the illustrious part of his career. Jessica Tandy's desparate, shrill, terrified Blanche and Kim Hunter's contented sister were sharply imagined and acted, and the baleful moods rose and fell in the acting of a perfectly balanced cast. The audience was both moved and elated by the performance, and *A Streetcar Named Desire* received both the Pulitzer Prize and the Critics Circle Award.[2]

That stage production had great significance for the entire realm of naturalistic acting.

Throughout the fifties, the Method played a dominant role in realistic performances. As Walter Kerr noted, the Method evolved from the "low-keyed naturalism" of the Group Theatre in the thirties to the "open fire" of the Actors Studio in the fifties, from "prosy accuracy" to "rhythmic power" that was fully appropriate for the plays of Tennessee Williams, Arthur Miller, and William Inge, "our best young playwrights."[3]

Throughout the 1950s, the psychoanalytic style remained dominant in commercial theatre, although a substantial undercurrent of experimentation with nonrealism occurred in the latter part of the decade. That wave of nonrealism had a telling effect on the use of the Method on stage.

In the fifties, the off-Broadway theatre movement was popularized, and low-budget experimental works were mounted. The experimental vogue was more fully realized a decade later when off-Broadway and off-off-Broadway departed even further from the mainstream of commercialism and realism. The experimental stage exploited the environmental uniqueness of theatre, that is, the presence of the live actor and audience. In this context, theatre experimented with "happenings" (using very few actors), theatre games, improvisational techniques, and transformational techniques.

The exploitation of actor-audience relationships resulted in a theatre of kinetic energy and sensory assault. Groups such as the Living Theatre, organized by Julian Beck and Judith Malina, developed a ritualistic style in which actors communicated through physical and sensory expressions rather than through the polemic of the word. The idea was conceived by Antonin Artaud, whose *Theatre and Its Double* (1958) became the manifesto for the Theatre of Cruelty. As opposed to the Stanislavski concept of analyzing the text and character, Artaud sought to purge the senses of the audience through assault; his actors became animated hieroglyphics, using metaphysical breathing to break the constraints of traditional language, with no reliance upon a written text or character.

In contrast to the realistic work done at the Actors Studio, experimentalists like Joseph Chaiken saw the need for actors to be retrained in nonrealistic techniques. Chaiken's Open Theatre was developed specifically to help actors deal with the new experimentation. Chaiken himself was influenced by Stanislavski's techniques, but experimented with kinetic responses in sound and movement, and the shifting of roles through time, space, and action:

> The Method actor gets tied up in the character's psychological knots, but in the new theatre he keeps up his awareness that he's an actor on stage. Instead of portraying an individual he's a universal man.[4]

The influence of Stanislavski on experimental theatre practitioners should not go unnoticed. The system affected the most prominent nonrealists, including Brecht, Meyerhold, Vakhtangov, and Grotowski. Each felt that Stanislavski's principles were practical and flexible in their pursuit of new artistic forms. Grotowski, for example, wrote:

> I was brought up on Stanislavski; his persistent study, his systematic renewal of the methods of observation, and his dialectical relationship to his own earlier work make him my personal ideal. Stanislavski asked the key methodological questions. Our solutions, however, differ widely from his—sometimes we reach opposite conclusions.[5]

Jerzy Grotowski felt that the war between theatre and film had been waged and lost. The stage could not compete with motion pictures and television for naturalism. "No matter how much theatre expands and exploits its mechanical resources, it will remain technologically inferior to film and television. Consequently, I propose poverty in theatre."[6] The "poor theatre" proposed by Grotowski exploited the inherent nature of the art form, stripped of extraneous detail. Instead of seeking a theatre of cinematic technique, he preached a theatre of magic and ritualism, with transformed spatial relationships and universal archetypes as characters. The Grotowski actor played himself, rather than a "traditional role"; he created facial masks through physical techniques alone, and sought a mystical experience involving himself and the audience.

After the sixties, theatre remained divided between the commercial offerings of Broadway and regional theatre, and the noncommercial experimentation of off-Broadway and off-off-Broadway. The Broadway stage and regional theatre experienced a void in the contributions of new realistic playwrights. Edward Albee and Neil Simon were among the few major playwrights to emerge in this period.

With such intensive experimentation going on in the theatre, the Method was considered inappropriate for many of the nonrealistic production companies. As a deliberate challenge, Elia Kazan staged a nonrealistic production of *The Changeling* (1964), by Thomas Middleton and William Rowley, at the Lincoln Center. The reviews were scathing. The performance was criticized for its lack of ensemble effectiveness, and the show was considered an artistic disaster. In the wave of ensuing criticism, Kazan resigned from the Lincoln Center, along with another executive, Robert Whitehead:

> No doubt audiences expected too much, for an ensemble cannot be built overnight. But *The Changeling* also pinpointed the weaknesses of American Method acting, which had concentrated almost entirely on modern, realistic drama. The failure of this production was crucial in the widespread disenchantment with the "Method" during the late 1960s.[7]

In contrast to the nonrealism of theatre experimentation, motion pictures and television remained largely naturalistic. The techniques of the Method were fully appropriate for the cinematic medium, where realistic acting prevailed.

Hollywood in the Fifties and Sixties

During this period, feature films were largely based on adapted material. Unlike the films of the forties, when studio writers developed hordes of original material, the fifties and sixties saw a shift to screen adaptations based on previously successful works. Producers turned out films based on popular books and plays, such as *From Here to Eternity* (1953), *The Caine Mutiny* (1954), *Not as a Stranger* (1955), *Tea and Sympathy* (1956), *Marjorie Morningstar* (1958), *Exodus* (1960), *Sweet Bird of Youth* (1961). One historan aptly called the period "the Age of Adaptations."[8]

Inherent in the use of adaptations was the promise of sexual themes and strong character conflicts. Although the motion picture industry adhered to a censorship code—The Breen Code of 1934—it was considerably less restrictive than the television code that prohibited depictions of sex, violence, and any deviation from acceptable norms. Consequently, studios hoped to lure television audiences to the box office with sexual themes, social criticism, and antiheroes.[9]

Although the features dealt with strong subject manner, they skirted graphic depictions of sex or violence. Characters and dramatic action operated within the relatively tame confines of the censorship code. Passions were underlying themes for many films of the period, but those passions could only be suggested on screen. Some of the typical films in this cycle were *Peyton Place* (1957), based on a best-seller about sex, frustration, and violence in a small New England town; *Butterfield 8* (1960), based on John O'Hara's novel about the personal life of a call girl; *Splendor in the Grass* (1961), by William Inge, about adolescent lovers in a small Kansas town; and *Summer and Smoke* (1961), based on Tennessee William's play about the unrequited passions of a minister's daughter in a small Mississippi town.

Given the dramatic interplay in the film scripts of the period, actors had substantial opportunity to delve into analytic characterizations. Critics praised the naturalism in film acting, and several of the films of the fifties won multiple best acting awards. *All About Eve* (1953), *From Here to Eternity* (1953), and *On the Waterfront* (1954) were ranked among the most often nominated films for best acting awards.[10]

Gordon Gow, in his study of Hollywood films of the fifties, recounted the dramatic impact of screen acting in the period, associating it historically with Stanislavski:

> The fifties saw an important development in screen acting. It was not without precedent. It was a progression from the mime of Lillian Gish, who certainly identified with the characters she played. More emphatically, it derived from the precept of Constantin Stanislavski... "You must live the part every moment you are playing it." For half a century Stanislavski's theories were known to many actors and teachers. Michael Chekhov, who had worked with him in Russia, went to Hollywood in the Forties, where he acted in movies (among them

Hitchcock's *Spellbound*) and imparted much knowledge to his students there. But the name of Stanislavski impinged freshly, and in some cases too astringently for comfort . . . the year Marlon Brando . . . appeared as Stanley Kowalski [in *A Streetcar Named Desire*]. This play was the making of him. His performance drew the town, praise for it echoed around the world, and Hollywood took notice. As a corollary, word also spread that the secret of Brando's success was due in no small measure to improvisational sessions at the Actors Studio in New York.[11]

Elia Kazan had the most pronounced impact on the use of the Method in films of the period. It was his work with Marlon Brando in *A Streetcar Named Desire* (1951) that focused new attention on the techniques of the Actors Studio and the use of the Method in film. This film seemed to characterize the power of Method acting on screen. Kazan had the analytic complexities of the character in mind when he cast Brando in the stage and film versions:

I think one of the best things I did for the play was to cast Brando in it—Brando has the vulgarity, the cruelty, and sadism—and at the same time he has something terribly attractive about him. So you can understand a woman [like Blanche Dubois] playing affectionately with an animal that's going to kill her. . . Thinking about that helped me clarify for myself my own feelings about the ambiguity in character. . . Hate turns to love and both are expressed in action. This is all through my films.[12]

When Kazan transferred the play to film, he used the Method to work with his actors.[13] He based his approach strictly on Stanislavski, first analyzing the structure of the play, then building each scene through awareness of that analytic structure. Sounding very much like Boleslavski on the use of dramatic action in film, he explained:

The idea [of] the Method was to consider the play like the trunk of a tree with the branches coming out and you had a branch that led you to another branch and slowly you came to the first climax of the play which contained the theme. The idea was that if you performed all the tasks on the way you would be able to perform the tasks at the end. We used to refer to it as the spine with all the vertebrae coming off it. So when I was preparing films I also tried to capture in a phrase what the essential task was, to sum it up in one sentence.[14]

The Method also gave him a way of defining the psychological progress of characters he directed on film. Kazan identified basic elements of the Stanislavski system that he found particularly valuable in his work as a film director:

There's a basic element in the Stanislavski system that has always helped me a lot in directing actors in the movies. The key word, if I had to pick one, is "to want." We used to say in the theatre: "What are you on stage *for*? What do you walk on stage to get? What do you want?" I always asked that of my actors; what they're in the scene to obtain; to achieve. . . . Another thing in the Stanislavski system that I always stress a lot when I direct the actors is what happened just before the scene. I not only talk about it, I sometimes improvise it. By the time the scene starts, they're fully in it, not just saying the lines they've been given.[15]

With the impact of Kazan's films and Brando's performances, the Method became widely known for psychoanalytic naturalism of characters in conflict. Its popularity, however, was accompanied by substantial controversy. Method actors were accused of being dogmatic, elite, and self-indulgent. Robert Lewis, for example, charged them with making "fetishes" of certain aspects of the Stanislavski system:

> They have created a new style of ham acting. . . . They are recognizable by a certain stance, certain gestures, and certain tones or *non*-tones. Their characteristic behavior in itself has become a style which limits the artist instead of freeing him, as a technique should.[16]

The same attitude was expressed by Vladimir Sokolov, a noted actor who worked with Stanislavski:

> It is sad and disappointing to watch those "Method-ists" acting. Every individuality has been leveled by the cliche—"Method" to an inarticulate performance in speech and expression. See one, see all.[17]

The image of the "inaudible," "slovenly," "arrogant" Method actor was symbolized by Marlon Brando's mumbling, angry, introspective characters in films such as *A Streetcar Named Desire* (1951), *On the Waterfront* (1954), and *The Wild One* (1957). The same rebellious nature was captured by another Actors Studio member, James Dean, in *Rebel Without a Cause* (1955), *East of Eden* (1955), and *Giant* (1955). Together, they epitomized the indulgent stereotype associated with the Actors Studio.

Ironically, James Dean was not one of the more active members of the Studio. After passing his audition in 1952, he prepared a scene for critique, and Strasberg harshly criticized his work. Afterward, he rarely returned to the Studio. Still, he considered the Studio a vital place for growth as an actor, and used its techniques for his film characterizations.[18]

The Method approach to acting was the most effective and penetrating style for the times. Tennessee Williams, Arthur Miller, and William Inge dominated the serious stage; the films of Elia Kazan, Marlon Brando, and James Dean represented the mainstream of motion pictures. In *The Wild One* (1957), Brando's character wavers between aggressiveness and awkwardness, trying to compensate for his father's brutal treatment of him as a child. In *Rebel Without a Cause* (1955), Dean's character is in the throes of adolescent conflict, playing inner turmoil against the broader conflict of the generation gap. The intense psychoanalytic approach of the Actors Studio strove for a more naturalistic approach to creating a role, and a deeper grasp of the internally afflicted characters of many current dramatic works.

In this vein, Thomas R. Atkins distinguished the Method film actor of the fifties from the earlier actors of the thirties and forties:

Brando, Montgomery Clift, Julie Harris, Eli Wallach, Patricia Neal, Kim Hunter, Anthony Perkins, Rod Steiger, and the other Method performers who emerged in the fifties are best in divided parts based on the unresolved tension between an outer social mask and an inner reality of frustration.... In contrast, the popular roles played by earlier actors such as Spencer Tracy, Humphrey Bogart, Katherine Hepburn, James Cagney, Bette Davis, or Frederic March seem exceptionally well-integrated and direct.[19]

The earlier film actors had no pragmatic need for developing analytic dimensions to their character. The fundamental precepts of acting realism were sufficient to provide an interesting and dynamic performance without the subtleties and complexities of inner conflict. Katherine Cornell, for example, felt that emotional memory and personal substitution of experiences were totally unnecessary for the actor. She stressed imagination as the key to acting; all the rest was a "waste of time." As for her perception of Lee Strasberg at the Actors Studio: "He might say that's why I'm not a very good actress."[20]

In films of the sixties, the characters were still caught between social and personal conflicts, but the actors now portrayed more identifiable heroes and antiheroes. This was the era of Dustin Hoffman's anxiety-ridden college student in *The Graduate* (1967), Jack Nicholson's dropout cyclist in *Easy Rider* (1969), Joanne Woodward's anguished matron in *Rachel, Rachel* (1968), and Rod Steiger's intense survivor in *The Pawnbroker* (1965).

Rod Steiger played a range of roles over the years, including Al Capone, Napolean, Mussolini, W.C. Fields, a schizophrenic Irish poet, a Mafia don. He worked opposite Brando in *On the Waterfront* (1954), and played a Jewish survivor of the concentration camps in *The Pawnbroker* (1965). Throughout the decade he relied upon the Method to help create naturalistic performances. Steiger felt that the Actors Studio allowed him to experiment as an actor, to find the truth of a character, that he conveyed on screen.[21]

However, Hollywood was not in a stable enough position to support a great many artistic experiments. The motion picture studios experienced severe financial hardship in the late fifties and sixties. They suffered from relentless competition from television and from extraordinary escalation of production costs. During the 1950s, feature production was cut back almost fifty percent, and the number of staff writers, actors, and directors declined to less than two hundred (compared to fourteen hundred contract staff in 1945).[22] During the sixties, only one hundred sixty-three films were produced, compared to more than three hundred seventy in the fifties, and more than four hundred fifty in the forties.[23]

Studios were desperate in the sixties. The average cost of a feature production climbed to $3 million by 1966, and box office figures continued to plummet downward. In the midst of that financial crunch, one big-budget musical was released, *The Sound of Music* (1965), which grossed more than $135 million at the box office. In a desperate attempt to repeat that success and to capitalize on perceived audience interest, the studios committed large sums of money for the production of big-budget musicals and spectacles. Twentieth Century Fox committed millions of dollars to films such as *Dr. Doolittle* (1967), *Star* (1968), and *Tora! Tora! Tora!* (1970); the latter film was budgeted at $25 million. Similarly, Paramount Pictures turned out *Paint Your Wagon* (1969) for $20 million, *Darling Lili* (1970) for $19 million, and *The Molly McGuires* (1970) for $17 million. But the audiences were unresponsive, the box office floundered, and the studios suffered devastating losses. In 1969, 20th Century Fox found itself with more than $300 million in inventory, and more than $30 million in losses.[24]

While the studios were competing in the high-stakes gamble of major spectacles, a few smaller-budgeted films began to show profits at the box office. The unknown actor Dustin Hoffman starred in *The Graduate* (1967); Faye Dunaway and Warren Beatty starred in *Bonnie and Clyde* (1967). Both films won critical acclaim and earned substantial profits. A short time later, *Easy Rider* (1969) was independently produced for under $500,000, and returned an extraordinary profit of more than $50 million at the box office. The film featured two unknown actors, Jack Nicholson and Dennis Hopper.

Despite the success of these smaller-budgeted films, it was too late for the studios to reshape their commitment to high budget spectacles. As a result, the financial losses were critical. Forced to re-examine their position in the motion picture industry, the studios began to rent facilities to independent producers, sell their back lots to real estate developers, open up tourist attractions, shelve their films, and join forces with television production companies and syndicators. Many were taken over by corporate conglomerates.[25]

With the collapse of the major studios, the independent producer emerged as the dominant creative force in the industry. By the mid-sixties, eighty percent of all films made in the United States were independently produced.[26] As independent producers turned out smaller films, a significant new trend evolved in the casting of actors: unknown actors were featured in lead roles. Dustin Hoffman's appearance in *The Graduate* (1967) opened the door for other "ordinary looking" people with natural credibility. One critic called it the "era of new faces": Jack Nicholson, Richard Benjamin, Donald Sutherland, Jon Voight, Gene Wilder, Elliot Gould, Woody Allen. As those new actors created identifiable characters in different films, the need for star appeal diminished: "A pattern was beginning to appear. Star mystique was no longer vital as the film itself became the main attraction. Actor and actress adaptability in the total context of a film became the crucial element."[27]

Dustin Hoffman showed great versatility as an actor, moving from adolescent turbulence in *The Graduate* (1967) to the pits of the bowery in *Midnight Cowboy* (1969). Hoffman has maintained that his adaptability as an actor is the direct result of his Method training.[28] According to Hoffman, it was his work with Strasberg that stretched him into such versatile roles:

I was very affected by Lee Strasberg when I studied with him; he would say over and over again, 'There is no such thing as a juvenile or an ingenue or a villain or a hero or a leading man. We're all characters.'... It hit me very strong, because I was a victim of casting.[29]

After his role as the returning college student, Benjamin, in *The Graduate* (1967), he purposely sought a contrasting role to counter the impression that he was simply playing himself on screen:

I was out to show that I was a character actor—and that Benjamin was as much a character as any part I had done—and that I was not just the nebbish kid that Mike Nichols [the director] found.[30]

When he decided to play the part of the crippled derelict in *Midnight Cowboy* (1969), Mike Nichols tried to dissuade him on the grounds that it was an unattractive character, a secondary role, and might demean the career he had established in his previous film.[31] His portrayal won Hoffman the Best Supporting Actor nomination in the Academy Awards.

The use of "real-looking" people in film roles versus star actors, peaked in the sixties. The use of the Method had contributed to the escalating conflict between the two practices.

During this period, the analytic characterizations of Brando and Dean from the fifties were superceded by more identifiable, adaptable characters portrayed by Dustin Hoffman, Jack Nicholson, and Al Pacino. In essence, the psychoanalytic portrayals gave way to the importance of themes suggested in the film. Elia Kazan saw that shift in his own work over the years:

I'm not as interested in the minutiae, in the small psychological turns, as I used to be—I'm interested in broader strokes now. I don't explain everything as I used to, I'm not psychologizing so much... What gets better now is my themes... I don't want you to watch how flashy this performance is, I want you to think about what's really going on.[32]

Because of that shift, Stanislavski's emphasis on dramatic action, from the days of Nazimova, Boleslavski, and Ouspenskaya, seemed to be preserved intact in the Hollywood years of the late twentieth century.

The Heritage: American Film Acting, 1970-1980s

Hollywood in the Seventies and Eighties

During the seventies and eighties, some of the most expensive films of all time were produced, including multi-million dollar epics such as *The Godfather I, II* (1972, 1974), *Star Wars* (1977), *Jaws I, II* (1976, 1978), *Close Encounters of the Third Kind* (1977), *Superman I, II* (1978, 1980), *Star Trek* (1979), *Moonraker* (1979), *Apocalypse Now* (1979), *Flash Gordon* (1980), *The Empire Strikes Back* (1980), *Heaven's Gate* (1980), *Raiders of the Lost Ark* (1983), *Indiana Jones and the Temple of Doom* (1984), and *Gremlins* (1984). The trend toward big-budget features continued unabated, with production costs soaring to an average of $11.6 million by 1984.[1]

Once again it was the hope of the motion picture industry that large-scale production values would generate unbridled enthusiasm at the box office. Some of those films did pay off, ranking among the highest-grossing films of all times.[2] However, most did not earn back their extravagant production costs. Perhaps the epitome of high stakes recklessness was Michael Cimino's *Heaven's Gate* (1980), which was released by United Artists, and cost $35 million to produce. A sprawling tale of cattle barons who fought immigrants in the 1890s, the film was lambasted by critics and the public. *Variety* summed up the reactions of critics and the Hollywood community:

> (It) is so confusing, so overlong...so ponderous, that it fails at almost every level.... The trade must marvel that directors now have such power that no one, in the endless months since work on the picture began, was able to impose some structure and sense.[3]

The power of the independent producer and director reigned supreme. The period nurtured some of America's most innovative filmmakers, including Peter Bogdanovich, Steven Spielberg, Francis Ford Coppola, Martin Scorsese, and George Lucas. Some of their films featured outstanding visual effects and production atmosphere to bring audiences back into the movie theatres. Several of those efforts succeeded beyond anyone's expectations, for example, *Star Wars* (1977), *E.T.* (1982), and *Raiders of the Lost Ark* (1983). Others, such as *1941* (1979) and *Twilight Zone: The Movie* (1984) suffered unpredictable failures and setbacks.

While Hollywood continued to spawn high budget special effects features, a countertrend was established with smaller, issue-oriented films. Many of these films touched a responsive chord with the public, and offered significant opportunities for casting "ordinary" character types. In his history of motion pictures, Gerald Mast suggests that a new cultural attitude was reflected in these films:

> The rebels, misfits, loners, and oddballs that dominated American film from *Bonnie and Clyde* (1967) through *Taxi Driver* (1976) have been replaced by more ordinary citizens who seek to find a meaningful place for themselves within conventional American society.[4]

Themes of nostalgia, social consciousness, and coming of age were explored on screen in the seventies and eighties; actors portrayed realistic people in recognizable situations. These domestic dramas required the ultimate in naturalistic acting. *Coming Home* (1978) dealt with problems faced by a disabled Vietnam War veteran (Jon Voight) trying desperately to adjust to life back in the states. The film won acclaim for Actors Studio members Jane Fonda, "another memorable and moving performance;" Jon Voight, "assured and effective;" and Bruce Dern, "continuing to forge new career dimensions."[5]

In *Kramer vs. Kramer* (1979), Dustin Hoffman played a single father struggling for the right to live with his son. Critics praised the dimensionality of the character, and the naturalistic performances on screen.[6]

Another film, *Ordinary People* (1980), examined the impact of a son's death on the surviving family members (Mary Tyler Moore, Donald Sutherland, Timothy Hutton). The picture, directed by Robert Redford, won critical praise for its naturalistic impact. It has been called "a powerful intimate domestic drama... An actor's picture."[7] Another actor's picture was *On Golden Pond* (1981), depicting the familial relationships between an aging patriarch (Henry Fonda), his wife (Katherine Hepburn), and his daughter (Jane Fonda). All were cited for distinguished performances by the press and the Motion Picture Academy.

Those themes of friendship and social relationships continued to proliferate with identifiable characters and naturalistic acting at the core of films such as *Four Seasons* (1982), Alan Alda's tribute to friendship; *The Big Chill* (1983), which reunited college friends after the suicide of one of their friends; and *Terms of Endearment* (1983), which merged three decades of family relationships and friendships into a single story, winning awards for Jack Nicholson and Shirley MacLaine.

Themes of social consciousness and identity awareness distinguished these domestic dramas, and allowed a wide range of performances by actors trained in the Method and other interpretations of the Stanislavski system. The Actors Studio alone boasted a strong record of achievement, with more than seventy nominations for best acting awards in the Motion Picture Academy competition from 1970 to 1984. Studio members have historically done well in the eyes of their peers. As of 1984, more than one hundred and fifty Academy Award nominations and thirty-five Awards have gone to Studio members. (For a list of Studio members who have won Academy Award nominations, see Appendix A.)

In the annual Golden Globe competition, foreign journalists representing over fifty countries vote on the most outstanding performances in drama and comedy; they also honor achievements in television drama. The seventies and eighties have been rich in Golden Globe Awards for members of the Actors Studio: Marlon Brando, Dustin Hoffman, Walter Matthau, Paul Newman, Jack Nicholson, Al Pacino, Maureen Stapleton, Shelley Winters, Jane Fonda, and Sally Field. (For a list of Studio members who have won Golden Globe Awards, see Appendix C.)

Similarly, the Academy of Television Arts and Sciences has consistently nominated a large number of Studio members for their work in television films, miniseries, specials, and series. Among those repeatedly nominated in the seventies and eighties were Lee Grant, Beatrice Arthur, Cloris Leachman, Marlon Brando, Karl Malden, Julie Harris, Rosemary Murphy, Nancy Marchand, Patricia Neal, Carroll O'Connor, Ralph Waite, Dennis Weaver, Paul Winfield, and Joanne Woodward.[8]

Awards by the Motion Picture Academy, the Golden Globes, or the Academy of Television Arts and Sciences are not the sole criteria for success. However, the strong pattern of national recognition by peers and critics implies a significant and distinctive contribution to the art of American film acting by many Actors Studio members.

The Actors Studio West

Given the large number of Hollywood actors and directors exposed to the Method, it was not surprising that they would want to establish a West Coast branch of the Actors Studio. In response to that need, Dennis Weaver gave a reception for studio members who lobbied for a West Coast branch (1965). Finally Lee Strasberg agreed to oversee its development and approved plans to move ahead. The Actors Studio West received more than one hundred twenty applications for membership, but only seven people passed the final audition. With that small nucleus, it became apparent that the Studio needed to bolster its membership, and they subsequently invited observers. Among those invited to participate as observers were Jack Albertson, Elizabeth Ashley, Candice Bergen, Red Buttons, Diahann Carroll, Patty Duke, Richard Dreyfuss, Mary Tyler Moore, Sally Field, Jack Nicholson, and Raquel Welch.[9]

The use of celebrities as observers and invited members is characteristic of the Studio's drive toward prominence in motion pictures. However, questions are raised concerning the actual activities of the participants, the audition process, and the criteria for selection of members. Many of the actors in observer status simply watched the workshop exercises of others. Red Buttons, for example, recalls his invitation to observe; it was a session in which actors prepared scenes and members critiqued them.[10] Similarly, other actors have discussed the "nonparticipatory" roles they played as observers.[11]

The roster of the Studio has been confusing over the years, presenting another problem in assessing the extent of Method impact on film actors. Until the advent of the Studio Theatre in the sixties, a complete list of life members was not available, and provisional membership was a transitional category. As of 1984, the Studio had a list of nearly six hundred and fifty names, and it is impossible to determine the criteria for selection of that membership.[12]

According to the Actors Studio, most actors prepare a scene for audition, but as David Garfield notes, there are a great number of exceptions. During the fifties, actors of "a certain status" were invited to become active members. In the sixties, Studio Theatre actors were admitted, and so were prominent theatre and film actors, directors, and playwrights. In the seventies, Strasberg invited other film and television actors to join, including Jill Clayburgh, Robert De Niro, Robert Duvall, Lainie Kazan, Michael Moriarity, Jack Nicholson, and Carroll O'Connor. In the eighties, motion picture and television actors were continuously asked to participate on an ad hoc basis at the Studio.

For that reason, the list of members may be misleading. One actor, José Ferrer, asserted that most of the "big names" went to the Method after they had established themselves, not before.[13] Dustin Hoffman, who joined the Studio in 1966, was consistently denied membership until he was celebrated on screen, although he studied privately with Strasberg.[14] Other actors were invited by Strasberg to study and work at the Studio after they had already achieved film status; many never took advantage of that opportunity.[15]

Robert Duvall, who is listed as a Studio member, has publicly dissociated himself from the Studio and Strasberg:

> When I'm on, I think I operate as truthfully as any Method actor I know... But the word "Method" makes me think of Lee Strasberg, and I'm just not a disciple of that whole thing, although I think he knows a lot about the theatre.[16]

Still, the impact of the Method on film has been significant, and many members of the Studio have benefitted from exposure to the system. Paul Newman credited everything he knows about acting to the Studio.[17] Dustin Hoffman credited the Method for instilling concentration and control in all his work.[18] Sidney Poitier used the method in preparation for all his film roles.[19]

Maureen Stapleton claimed the Method instilled a sense of spontaneity in her performances.[20] Jane Fonda asserted that she was reluctant to follow in the career of her father, Henry Fonda, until she studied with Lee Strasberg at the Actors Studio; she found the Method "profoundly liberating."[21] Shelley Winters considered the Studio the most valuable resource for acting training in this country.[22]

When Lee Strasberg died in 1982, the Actors Studio was faced with a major challenge in its administrative structure and teaching philosophy. The Studio reaffirmed its intent to continue providing Method training for professional actors, but now the Studio was under the joint stewardship of two artistic directors, Ellen Burstyn and Al Pacino. The president of the board was Paul Newman, and the executive committee consisted of Elia Kazan, Arthur Penn, Estelle Parsons, Martin Landau, Sidney Pollack, and Mark Rydell. Members of the administration held various views of the changes the Studio faced. Martin Landau strongly believed that the Studio would become a national repertory theatre. Terry Moore, a trustee, expected an international impact, with branches of the Studio in different parts of the world. Sidney Pollack expected the Studio to continue the same work undertaken by Lee Strasberg.[23] The Studio has been an important vehicle for motion picture actors to explore the use of the Method, and it is likely that it will retain its influence, primarily through contacts, exposure, and experimentation.

Elements of the Stanislavski system are also widely used by a great number of actors, directors, and teachers outside the Studio. Acting teachers and professionals from New York to Los Angeles offer training in some aspects of script analysis and character development based on Stanislavski's ideas. The system demonstrated by Boleslavski and Ouspenskaya has continued to be used in various ways by Sanford Meisner, Stella Adler, Harold Clurman, Robert Lewis, Uta Hagen, and many others. The system in its later evolution has been particularly stressed by Sonia Moore. In short, variations of the original system are very much in use today, and the Method has been one modification that has met with particular success in American film.

Film Actors on Film Acting

The Method has provided a usable and practical framework for film actors, based on the early principles of Stanislavski. One Actors Studio member, Robert De Niro, who has been lauded for his "miraculous feats" as an actor, and his ability to "transform himself in his roles,"[24] meticulously used Method techniques for preparation and character development. In preparation for *Raging Bull* (1980), he spent months living the life of a boxer; for *The Deer Hunter* (1978), he lived among Ohio valley steel workers, observing their behavior and speech patterns. For *Bang the Drum Slowly* (1973) he observed how relaxed players seemed in every baseball game and "practiced in my room, watching them do nothing." In *The Last Tycoon* (1976), directed by Elia Kazan, he experimented with improvisations to find the nature of the character:

> We used to do improvs on the nature of being a studio executive...[Kazan's] method of improvisation doesn't mean improvising on the screen. It means improvising behind the scenes, like on a situation to find other colors...That's the way it's meant in the theatre—to loosen you up and find behavioral things...In movies, improvising means something else. It means you ad-lib, which can be o.k., too.[25]

De Niro studied with Lee Strasberg and Stella Adler, using all the traditional Stanislavski-based techniques, including character analysis, observation, affective memory, magic-if, and physicalization:

> The fun of it is when you get into just experimenting (with the full spectrum of techniques). If you're lucky, you make good choices that will work. As Stella Adler used to say, "your talent lies in your choice."[26]

Another Studio member, Dustin Hoffman, has been described in the *New York Times* as "one of America's finest and most popular actors...playing characters of remarkable diversity, giving unfailingly good performances."[27] Hoffman's use of the Method and his artistic confrontations with directors have become legendary. One film director said of him: "He's one of the most inventive actors I've ever known. He's so full of ideas that he almost gives too much. I loved working with him, but I'm not sure I'd want to do it again."[28] Hoffman relies heavily on observation, affective memory, role analysis, and improvisation. He approaches a role from the exploratory nature of improvisation, and embellishes with a full awareness of the character's inner life. He considers in-depth preparation indispensable for success in any film.[29]

Hoffman accuses some directors of being close-minded about the contributions an actor can make to a film, especially during preparation and collaborative phases of production. He improvised a great deal for his role in *Kramer vs. Kramer* (1979) and utilized affective memory exercises in preparation:

> The producer was Stanley Jaffe, the director-writer was Bob Benton. I had this part that was central to the story and the three of us worked on the script for months and we brought forth our own experiences. We argued, we talked, we fought—and out of it, I think, came a somewhat personal film by the three of us.[30]

According to Hoffman, they spent an intensive period of time on improvisational and affective memory techniques to heighten insight into the role. Hoffman's next film, *Tootsie* (1982) was largely based on an extended period of improvisation to explore the complexities of an actor subsumed by the female character he plays. The improvisational period extended over a three year period, involving playwright Murray Schisgal, Larry Gelbart, and Elaine May, who wrote the later script, and Sidney Pollack, who directed. Still, Hoffman complained that there was not enough time to rehearse, and that the screenplay wasn't completed before production commenced.[31]

Hoffman observed that artistic goals established in acting training are secondary to the realities of filmmaking:

> You study acting until you're blue in the face and you get out there and it's got nothing to do with what you studied: 'Here's your script, here are your lines, here's your mark, hit that, hit that, do this—and that's it. Good bye and good luck.'.. If only they would give you the time—but they don't... I wish I could convince them... that doing your work in advance—even if that preparation takes longer—will save time and money in the end, and more important, will give you far better odds of success.[32]

Jane Fonda also commented on the frustration of moving from the intensity and artistry of the Actors Studio to the pragmatics of filmmaking:

> When I was in New York at acting school, I was playing wonderful scenes and parts and just thoroughly enjoying the experience of acting. Suddenly, Hollywood had nothing to do with that, and I hated it.[33]

She gradually gained control over the roles she would play, and created award winning performances in films with social themes such as *They Shoot Horses, Don't They* (1969), *Klute* (1971), *Coming Home* (1978), *China Syndrome* (1979), and *On Golden Pond* (1981).

In her role preparation, Fonda has used Method techniques for emotional involvement and characterization. Her use of affective memory techniques and personal substitution help involve her in the character's inner life: "The way I approach acting, you infuse your soul, your being, into what is on the page to bring it to life."[34]

Paul Newman, who studied with Lee Strasberg and at the Yale School of Drama, has been praised for his ability to convey "moment-to-moment realities, allowing his own emotions to carry him in major film roles."[35] Like the other Studio actors , Newman spends a great deal of time in preparation, including script analysis, observation, and character development. For one film, *Cool Hand Luke*, he lived in the Appalachian country, "immersed in the surroundings. I ended up traveling around with a tomato salesman to observe his patterns of speech and behavior."[36] According to his wife, Joanne Woodward, "his scripts are always full of notes, he writes everything down to analyze."[37] He works intellectually to find the truthfulness of his character's motivation and action, and then taps into "his emotional reservoir" with affective memory techniques. Director George Roy Hill commented: "He wants to analyze everything. After that, he loosens up and responds emotionally, truthfully, and in-depth."[37]

Joanne Woodward studied with Sanford Meisner, and finds that she works best from the logic of physical actions, before allowing emotions to intervene. She considers herself a character actress; critics acknowledge her "stunning ability" to play a wide range of roles effectively. According to Woodward, she first analyzes the physicality of the character to determine what the character looks like, then develops the emotional life of the character, focusing on the problems of inner life.[39]

Clearly, different actors approach the problem of creating a role in many different ways. Each finds something unique that will work in the search for physical and inner truth. The techniques available from the Method provide a logical system for that exploration. Some actors begin their preparation with analysis of the script and character, finding clues to the physicalization and behavioral realities. They can utilize observation techniques to pattern physical and verbal exploration of the character. Finally, they can internalize the behavioral realities through a mixture of personal substitution and affective memory techniques. The artistic tools are at their disposal; they can select the most appropriate techniques for each new challenge.

It should be emphasized that the Method is used *selectively*, as needed, by individual performers. That selection process has been described by Academy Award winning actor Red Buttons:

> A film actor has to be very discriminating in the techniques he uses. The key is to pick and choose. The Method may have some elements that work at one time, and not at another. You have to find the elements that work best in each role, and discard the rest. The end result should seem like no acting.[40]

Robert De Niro agrees with that philosophy. He commented on the need to select the most effective choices from the totality of the Method: "It's like anything else. In the beginning you learn the rules, and then you realize that the rules are there to use or not to use, and that there are millions of different ways of doing something."[41] He endorses Stella Adler's belief that an actor must make choices, and the final choice determines the effectiveness of the final performance. Similarly, Dustin Hoffman emphasized that choices and experimentation should be fully explored in the preparation stage, so that the end result seems natural, not "acted":

> I say actors shouldn't have to 'act.' The scene should be constructed in such a way that you don't have to ('act') . . . It should be there, like butter—all the work should have been done beforehand—so you don't have to sit there and jerk up emotions. It should flow.[42]

Consistent with that philosophy, David Garfield reports that "surprisingly few Studio members use every aspect of the Method in the manner or with the consistency" prescribed by Lee Strasberg.[43] Still, the adaptability of the system allows its continued use by actors, directors, and teachers across the country.

The Actors Studio has been a conspicuous presence in the mainstream of American film acting. Although its membership is relatively small, the Studio—through its members and observers—has tapped into the professional consciousness of film actors and directors. The Method and its various offshoots remain a practical and useful tool for many film actors. The Method has been particularly well suited to the needs of realism in film acting. Through its analytic interpretation of Stanislavski's ideas, the system provides a workable foundation for achieving inner realism in close-up acting, and exacting a personal intimacy in a style that has responded to the needs of dramatic themes and characters portrayed in many films of recent decades.

Several key elements of the Stanislavski system have remained intact since the early days of Stanislavski's search for realism in a naturalistic environment. The core experience of acting remains based on the original concept of imagination directed toward the given circumstances of the script. The Method later emphasized the corollary experience of emotions derived from the personal life of the actor.

The film actor's approach to a role remains consonant with those developmental techniques established by Stanislavski: *intellectual work,* i.e., analyzing the script and character in depth; *inner work,* i.e., exploring the use of emotional recall, imagination, observation, concentration, and sensory awareness; and *outer technique,* i.e., physicalizing the character through body movement and voice. The end result is an effective, unified expression of all psychological and physical behavior.

The Stanislavski system provided a solid framework for actors to achieve truthful performances on stage and screen through analytical, emotional, and physical techniques. It has been interpreted in many ways over the years, and—largely through the Method—influenced the course of American film acting. The Method and other variations of the system have been absorbed into the mainstream of cinema, serving as the creative catalyst for experimentation by many of America's most distinguished actors, directors, and teachers. Given the historical roots of the system and the naturalistic requirements of cinema, it is likely that the system will continue to have a decisive influence on the future of American film.

Appendix A

Academy Award Nominations for Actors Studio Members

Year	Member	Motion Picture	Category (*Denotes winner)
1947	Celeste Holm	*Gentleman's Agreement*	Best Supporting Actress
	Elia Kazan	*Gentleman's Agreement*	*Best Director
1948	Montgomery Clift	*The Search*	Best Actor
1949	Celeste Holm	*Come to the Stable*	Best Supporting Actress
	James Whitmore	*The Battleground*	Best Supporting Actor
1950	Celeste Holm	*All About Eve*	Best Supporting Actress
1951	Marlon Brando	*A Streetcar Named Desire*	Best Actor
	Montgomery Clift	*A Place in the Sun*	Best Actor
	Mildred Dunnock	*Death of a Salesman*	Best Supporting Actress
	Kim Hunter	*A Streetcar Named Desire*	*Best Supporting Actress
	Elia Kazan	*A Streetcar Named Desire*	Best Director
	Karl Malden	*A Streetcar Named Desire*	*Best Supporting Actor
	Kevin McCarthy	*Death of a Salesman*	Best Supporting Actor
	Shelley Winters	*A Place in the Sun*	Best Actress
1952	Marlon Brando	*Viva Zapata*	Best Actor
	Julie Harris	*Member of the Wedding*	Best Actress
	Terry Moore	*Come Back Little Sheba*	Best Supporting Actress
1953	Marlon Brando	*Julius Caesar*	Best Actor
	Montgomery Clift	*From Here to Eternity*	Best Actor
	Geraldine Page	*Hondo*	Best Supporting Actress
1954	Marlon Brando	*On the Waterfront*	*Best Actor
	Elia Kazan	*On the Waterfront*	*Best Director
	Karl Malden	*On the Waterfront*	Best Supporting Actor
	Eva Marie Saint	*On the Waterfront*	*Best Supporting Actress
	Rod Steiger	*On the Waterfront*	Best Supporting Actor

Year	Member	Motion Picture	Category (*Denotes winner)
1955	James Dean	*East of Eden*	Best Actor
	Elia Kazan	*East of Eden*	Best Director
	Jo Van Fleet	*East of Eden*	*Best Supporting Actress
1956	Carroll Baker	*Baby Doll*	Best Supporting Actress
	James Dean	*Giant*	Best Actor
	Mildred Dunnock	*Baby Doll*	Best Supporting Actress
	Anthony Perkins	*Friendly Persuasion*	Best Supporting Actor
1957	Marlon Brando	*Sayonara*	Best Actor
	Sidney Lumet	*Twelve Angry Men*	Best Director
	Joanne Woodward	*The Three Faces of Eve*	*Best Actress
1958	Paul Newman	*Cat on a Hot Tin Roof*	Best Actor
	Sidney Poitier	*The Defiant Ones*	Best Actor
	Maureen Stapleton	*Lonely Hearts*	Best Supporting Actress
1959	Shelley Winters	*Diary of Anne Frank*	*Best Supporting Actress
1960	Shirley Knight	*Dark at the Top of the Stairs*	Best Supporting Actress
1961	Montgomery Clift	*Judgment at Nuremberg*	Best Supporting Actor
	Paul Newman	*The Hustler*	Best Actor
	Geraldine Page	*Summer and Smoke*	Best Actress
	Jerome Robbins	*West Side Story*	*Best Director
1962	Anne Bancroft	*The Miracle Worker*	*Best Actress
	Shirley Knight	*Sweet Bird of Youth*	Best Supporting Actress
	Arthur Penn	*The Miracle Worker*	Best Director
	Frank Perry	*David and Lisa*	Best Director
	Geraldine Page	*Sweet Bird of Youth*	Best Actress
1963	Elia Kazan	*America, America*	Best Director
	Patricia Neal	*Hud*	*Best Actress
	Paul Newman	*Hud*	Best Actor
	Sidney Poitier	*Lillies of the Field*	*Best Actor
	Martin Ritt	*Hud*	Best Director
1964	Anne Bancroft	*The Pumpkin Eater*	Best Actress
	Kim Stanley	*Séance on a Wet Afternoon*	Best Actress
1965	Martin Balsam	*A Thousand Clowns*	*Best Supporting Actor
	Rod Steiger	*The Pawnbroker*	Best Actor
	Shelley Winters	*A Patch of Blue*	*Best Supporting Actress

Year	Member	Motion Picture	Category (*Denotes winner)
1966	Sandy Dennis	*Who's Afraid of Virginia Woolf?*	*Best Supporting Actress
	Walter Matthau	*The Fortune Cookie*	*Best Supporting Actor
	Steve McQueen	*The Sand Pebbles*	Best Actor
	Geraldine Page	*You're a Big Boy Now*	Best Supporting Actress
1967	Anne Bancroft	*The Graduate*	Best Actress
	Dustin Hoffman	*The Graduate*	Best Actor
	Paul Newman	*Cool Hand Luke*	Best Actor
	Estelle Parsons	*Bonnie and Clyde*	Best Supporting Actress
	Arthur Penn	*Bonnie and Clyde*	Best Director
	Rod Steiger	*In the Heat of the Night*	*Best Actor
1968	Patricia Neal	*The Subject Was Roses*	Best Actress
	Estelle Parsons	*Rachel, Rachel*	Best Supporting Actress
	Cliff Robertson	*Charly*	*Best Actor
	Gene Wilder	*The Producers*	Best Supporting Actor
	Joanne Woodward	*Rachel, Rachel*	Best Actress
1969	Rupert Crosses	*The Reivers*	Best Supporting Actor
	Jane Fonda	*They Shoot Horses, Don't They?*	Best Actress
	Dustin Hoffman	*Midnight Cowboy*	Best Supporting Actor
	Sylvia Miles	*Midnight Cowboy*	Best Supporting Actress
	Jack Nicholson	*Easy Rider*	Best Supporting Actor
	Arthur Penn	*Alice's Restaurant*	Best Director
	Sidney Pollack	*They Shoot Horses, Don't They?*	*Best Director
	Jon Voight	*Midnight Cowboy*	Best Actor
1970	Lee Grant	*The Landlord*	Best Supporting Actress
	Sally Kellerman	*M*A*S*H*	Best Supporting Actress
	Jack Nicholson	*Five Easy Pieces*	Best Actor
	Maureen Stapleton	*Airport*	Best Supporting Actress
1971	Ellen Burstyn	*The Last Picture Show*	Best Supporting Actress
	Jane Fonda	*Klute*	*Best Actress
	Barbara Harris	*Harry Kellerman*	Best Supporting Actress
	Cloris Leachman	*The Last Picture Show*	*Best Supporting Actress
	Walter Matthau	*Kotch*	Best Actor
1972	Marlon Brando	*The Godfather*	*Best Actor
	Robert Duvall	*The Godfather*	Best Supporting Actor
	Al Pacino	*The Godfather*	Best Supporting Actor
	Geraldine Page	*Pete and Tillie*	Best Supporting Actress
	Paul Winfield	*Sounder*	Best Actor
	Shelley Winters	*The Poseidon Adventure*	Best Supporting Actress

Year	Member	Motion Picture	Category (*Denotes winner)
1973	Marlon Brando	*Last Tango in Paris*	Best Actor
	Ellen Burstyn	*The Exorcist*	Best Actress
	Vincent Gardenia	*Bang the Drum Slowly*	Best Supporting Actor
	Jack Nicholson	*Last Detail*	Best Actor
	Al Pacino	*Serpico*	Best Actor
	Joanne Woodward	*Summer Wishes, Winter Dreams*	Best Actress
1974	Ellen Burstyn	*Alice Doesn't Live Here Anymore*	*Best Actress
	Michael V. Gazzo	*The Godfather II*	Best Supporting Actor
	Dustin Hoffman	*Lenny*	Best Actor
	Diane Ladd	*Alice Doesn't Live Here Any More*	Best Supporting Actress
	Jack Nicholson	*Chinatown*	Best Actor
	Robert De Niro	*The Godfather II*	*Best Supporting Actor
	Al Pacino	*The Godfather II*	Best Actor
	Lee Strasberg	*The Godfather II*	Best Supporting Actor
1975	Lee Grant	*Shampoo*	*Best Supporting Actress
	Sidney Lumet	*Dog Day Afternoon*	Best Director
	Walter Matthau	*The Sunshine Boys*	Best Actor
	Burgess Meredith	*Day of the Locust*	Best Supporting Actor
	Sylvia Miles	*Farewell, My Lovely*	Best Supporting Actress
	Jack Nicholson	*One Flew Over the Cuckoo's Nest*	*Best Actor
	Al Pacino	*Dog Day Afternoon*	Best Actor
	James Whitmore	*Give 'em Hell, Harry*	Best Actor
1976	Robert De Niro	*Taxi Driver*	Best Actor
	Lee Grant	*Voyage of the Damned*	Best Supporting Actress
	Sidney Lumet	*Network*	Best Director
	Burgess Meredith	*Rocky*	Best Supporting Actor
	Beatrice Straight	*Network*	*Best Actress
1977	Anne Bancroft	*The Turning Point*	Best Actress
	Jane Fonda	*Julia*	Best Actress
1978	Ellen Burstyn	*Same Time Next Year*	Best Actress
	Jill Clayburgh	*An Unmarried Woman*	Best Actress
	Robert De Niro	*The Deer Hunter*	Best Actor
	Bruce Dern	*Coming Home*	Best Supporting Actor
	Jane Fonda	*Coming Home*	*Best Actress
	Geraldine Page	*Interiors*	Best Actress
	Maureen Stapleton	*Interiors*	Best Supporting Actress
	Jon Voight	*Coming Home*	*Best Actor
	Christopher Walken	*The Deer Hunter*	*Best Supporting Actor

Year	Member	Motion Picture	Category (*Denotes winner)
1979	Jill Clayburgh	*Starting Over*	Best Actress
	Robert Duvall	*Apocalypse Now*	Best Supporting Actor
	Sally Field	*Norma Rae*	*Best Actress
	Jane Fonda	*The China Syndrome*	Best Actress
	Dustin Hoffman	*Kramer vs. Kramer*	*Best Actor
	Al Pacino	*And Justice for All*	Best Actor
1980	Ellen Burstyn	*Resurrection*	Best Actress
	Robert De Niro	*Raging Bull*	*Best Actor
	Robert Duvall	*The Great Santini*	Best Actor
1981	Jane Fonda	*On Golden Pond*	Best Supporting Actress
	Paul Newman	*Absence of Malice*	Best Actor
	Jack Nicholson	*Reds*	Best Supporting Actor
	Maureen Stapleton	*Reds*	*Best Supporting Actress
1982	Dustin Hoffman	*Tootsie*	Best Actor
	Sidney Lumet	*The Verdict*	Best Director
	Paul Newman	*The Verdict*	Best Actor
	Sidney Pollack	*Tootsie*	Best Director
1983	Jane Alexander	*Testament*	Best Actress
	Robert Duvall	*Tender Mercies*	*Best Actor
	Jack Nicholson	*Terms of Endearment*	*Best Supporting Actor

Source: Files of the Actors Studio, New York.

Appendix B

Dates of Studio Membership
of Academy Award Nominees

Member	Date of Membership (If 1947, an original member)	Dates of Academy Nominations or Awards
Martin Balsam	1947	1965
Carroll Baker	1955	1956
Anne Bancroft	1958	1962, 1964, 1967, 1977
Marlon Brando	1947	1951, 1952, 1953, 1954, 1957, 1972,1973
Ellen Burstyn	1968	1971, 1973, 1974, 1978, 1980
Jill Clayburgh	1978	1979
Montgomery Clift	1947	1948, 1951, 1953, 1961
Rupert Crosse	1968	1970
James Dean	1952	1955, 1956
Robert De Niro	1974	1976, 1978, 1980
Sandy Dennis	1965	1966
Bruce Dern	1959	1978
Mildred Dunnock	1947	1951, 1956
Robert Duvall	1974	1972, 1980
Sally Field	1972	1979
Jane Fonda	1962	1969, 1971, 1977, 1978, 1979, 1981

Member	Date of Membership (If 1947, an original member)	Dates of Academy Nominations or Awards
Vincent Gardenia	1967	1973
Michael V. Gazzo	1953	1974
Lee Grant	n.d.	1970, 1975, 1976
Barbara Harris	1963	1971
Julie Harris	1947	1952
Dustin Hoffman	1966	1967, 1969, 1974, 1979, 1982
Celeste Holm	1964	1947, 1949, 1950
Kim Hunter	1947	1951
Elia Kazan	1947	1947, 1951, 1954, 1955, 1963
Sally Kellerman	1968	1970
Shirley Knight	1963	1960, 1962
Diane Ladd	1967	1974
Cloris Leachman	1947	1971
Sidney Lumet	1947	1957, 1975, 1976, 1982
Karl Malden	1947	1951, 1954
Walter Matthau	n.d.	1966, 1971, 1975
Steve McQueen	1956	1966
Burgess Meredith	1963	1975, 1976
Sylvia Miles	1968	1969, 1975
Terry Moore	1968	1952
Kevin McCarthy	1947	1951
Patricia Neal	1947	1968, 1963
Paul Newman	1947	1958, 1961, 1963, 1967, 1981, 1982

Member	Date of Membership (If 1947, an original member)	Dates of Academy Nominations or Awards
Jack Nicholson	1975	1969, 1970, 1973, 1974, 1975, 1981
Al Pacino	1966	1973, 1974
Geraldine Page	1956	1953, 1961, 1962, 1966, 1972, 1978
Estelle Parsons	1963	1967, 1968
Arthur Penn	1972	1962, 1967, 1969
Anthony Perkins	1963	1956
Frank Perry	1970	1962
Sidney Poitier	n.d.	1958, 1963
Sidney Pollack	n.d.	1969, 1982
Martin Ritt	n.d.	1963
Jerome Robbins	1947	1961
Cliff Robertson	1953	1968
Eva Marie Saint	1951	1954
Kim Stanley	1952	1964
Maureen Stapleton	1947	1958, 1970, 1978, 1981
Rod Steiger	1951	1954, 1965, 1967
Beatrice Straight	1947	1976
Lee Strasberg (Artistic Director)	1947	1974
Jo Van Fleet	1951	1955
Jon Voight	1983	1969, 1979
Christopher Walken	1977	1978
James Whitmore	1947	1949, 1975

Member	Date of Membership (If 1947, an original member)	Dates of Academy Nominations or Awards
Gene Wilder	1961	1968
Paul Winfield	1970	1972
Shelley Winters	n.d.	1951, 1959, 1965, 1972
Joanne Woodward	1956	1957, 1968, 1973

Source: Files of the Actors Studio, New York.

Member	Year	Title	Category
Kim Hunter	1951	*A Streetcar Named Desire*	Best Supporting Actress
Elia Kazan	1947	*Gentleman's Agreement*	Best Director
	1954	*On the Waterfront*	Best Director
	1956	*Cat on a Hot Tin Roof*	Best Director
	1963	*America, America*	Best Director
Cloris Leachman	1976	*Phyllis*	Best Actress
Tina Louise	1958	* *	Most Promising Newcomer
Kevin McCarthy	1951	*Death of a Salesman*	Best Supporting Actor
Steve McQueen	1966	* *	World Film Favorite
	1969	* *	World Film Favorite
Walter Matthau	1975	*The Sunshine Boys*	Best Actor
Paul Newman	1956	*Cat on a Hot Tin Roof*	Best Actor
	1963	*Hud*	Best Actor
	1965	* *	World Film Favorite
	1967	* *	World Film Favorite
	1968	*Butch Cassidy and The Sundance Kid*	Best Actor
	1983	* *	The Cecil B. DeMille Award
Jack Nicholson	1974	*Chinatown*	Best Actor
	1975	*One Flew Over the Cuckoo's Nest*	Best Actor
	1983	*Terms of Endearment*	Best Supporting Actor
Al Pacino	1973	*Serpico*	Best Actor
Geraldine Page	1961	*Summer and Smoke*	Best Actress
	1962	*Sweet Bird of Youth*	Best Actress
Anthony Perkins	1956	*Friendly Persuasion*	Best Supporting Actress
Sidney Poitier	1963	*A Raisin in the Sun*	Best Actor
	1968	* *	World Film Favorite
Maureen Stapleton	1970	*Airport*	Best Supporting Actress
Rod Steiger	1967	*In the Heat of the Night*	Best Actor
Jan Sterling	1954	*The High and the Mighty*	Best Supporting Actress
James Whitmore	1949	*The Battleground*	Best Supporting Actor
Shelley Winters	1972	*The Poseidon Adventure*	Best Actress

* * Special Category Winner.
Source: Files of the Actors Studio, New York.

Appendix C

Motion Picture/TV Golden Globe Awards for Actors Studio Members

Member	Year	Title	Category
Anne Bancroft	1964	*The Pumpkin Eater*	Best Actress
	1967	*The Graduate*	Best Actress
Marlon Brando	1954	*On the Waterfront*	Best Actor
	1955	*The Wild Ones*	Best Actor
	1972	*The Godfather*	Best Actor
	1973	*The Last Tango in Paris*	Best Actor
	1976	*Roots: The Second Generation*	Best Actor
Richard Beymar	1961	* *	Most Promising Newcomer
James Dean	1955	* *	Posthumous Award for Best Dramatic Actor
Bradford Dillman	1958	* *	Most Promising Newcomer
Keir Dullea	1962	* *	Most Promising Newcomer
Robert Duvall	1983	*Tender Mercies*	Best Actor
Tom Ewell	1955	*The Seven Year Itch*	Best Actor
Sally Field	1976	*Sybil*	Best Actress
	1979	*Norma Rae*	Best Actress
Jane Fonda	1977	*Julia*	Best Actress
	1981	*On Golden Pond*	Best Supporting Actress
John Forsythe	1959	* *	Most Promising Newcomer
Dustin Hoffman	1967	*The Graduate*	Best Actor
	1982	*Tootsie*	Best Actor
	1979	*Kramer vs. Kramer*	Best Actor
Celeste Holm	1947	*Gentleman's Agreement*	Best Supporting Actress

Notes

Introduction

1. Inez and Helen Klumph, *Screen Acting: Its Requirements and Rewards* (New York: Falk Publishing Co., 1922), pp. 87-88.

2. V.I. Pudovkin, *Film Technique and Film Acting*, trans. Ivor Montagu (London: Vision Press, 1954), 2: 116-17.

3. William K. Howard, "Stage and Screen Acting are Almost Alike," *New York World Telegram*, 21 January 1939.

4. Alexander Knox, "Acting and Behaving," *Hollywood Quarterly* (now *Film Quarterly*) I, No. 3 (Spring 1946): 260.

5. Eric Larrabee, Review of *Theory of Film* by Siegfried Kracauer, *Harper's*, January 1961, 31.

Chapter 1

1. Constantin Stanislavski, *My Life in Art*, trans. J.J. Robbins (New York: Theatre Arts, 1948), 570-71. KS, on filming actors to help their craft

2. Ibid., 383.

3. Ibid., 383-84.

4. Ibid., 569.

5. *K. Stanislavsky: 1863-1963, Man and Actor, Stanislavsky and the World Theatre, Stanislavsky's Letters*, trans. Vic Schneirson (Moscow: Progress Publishers, n.d., ca. 1964), 252. on

6. Ibid., 271.

7. Stanislavski, *My Life in Art*, 330.

8. For more on George II, Duke of Saxe-Meiningen, see Max Grube, *The Story of the Meiningen*, trans. Anne Marie Koller (Coral Gables, Florida: Univ. of Miami Press, 1963); Toby Cole and Helen Krich Chinoy, eds., *Directors on Directing* (New York: The Bobbs-Merrill Company, Inc., 1953, rev. 1963), 81-88.

9. Theodore Hoffman, "TDR Comment: Stanislavski Triumphant," *Tulane Drama Review*, 9, No. 1 (Fall 1964):#12.

10. Stanislavski, *My Life in Art*, 462-63.

11. Paul Gray, "Stanislavski and America: A Critical Chronology," *Tulane Drama Review*, 9, No. 2 (Winter 1964): #24; the typescript MS has been preserved in the M.A.T. Museum, Vzh 19, No. 1972, 44 pp.

12. Stanislavski, *My Life in Art*, 571.

13. Constantin Stanislavski, "The Art of the Actor and the Art of the Director," in *Stanislavski's Legacy*, ed. and trans. Elizabeth Reynolds Hapgood (New York: Theatre Arts Books, 1958), 170-82.

14. Nikolai Gorchakov, *Stanislavski Directs* (New York: The Universal Library, 1962), 119-21.

15. Talma, "Reflections on Acting," in *Papers on Acting*, ed. Brander Matthews (New York: Hill and Wang, 1958), 49.

16. David Magarshack, *Stanislavski, A Life* (New York: The Chanticleer Press, 1951), 343.

17. Stanislavski, "The Art of the Actor and the Art of the Director," 178.

18. Leslie Coger, "Stanislavski Changes His Mind," *Tulane Drama Review*, 9, No. 1 (Fall 1964), 63-68.

19. Lee Strasberg, Lecture at the Lee Strasberg Theatre Institute, Los Angeles, 14 May 1973.

20. Gorchakov, *Stanislavski Directs*, 193.

21. Lee Strasberg, "Strasberg vs. TDR," *Tulane Drama Review*, 11, No. 1 (Fall 1966): 234-39.

22. See for example, Suzanne O'Malley, "Can the Method Survive the Madness?," *New York Times Magazine*, 7 October 1979, 32.

23. For more on Meyerhold *see* B. Alpers, *The Theatre of the Social Mask*, trans. Mark Schmidt (New York: The Group Theatre, 1934); James M. Symons, *Meyerhold's Theatre of the Grotesque: The Post-Revolutionary Productions, 1920-1932* (Coral Gables: Univ. of Miami Press, 1971); Also of interest is Lee Strasberg, "The Magic Meyerhold," *New Theatre*, 1 (September 1934): 14-15, 30.

24. For more on Vakhtangov, *see* Nikolai Gorchakov, *The Vakhtangov School of Art* (New York: Theatre Arts Books, 1961); Ruben Simonov, *Stanislavsky's Protege: Eugene Vakhtangov*, trans. and adapted by Miriam Goldina (New York: Drama Book Specialists, 1969); Also cf. E. Vakhtangov, "Eugene Vakhtangov: 1833-1922," Diary Excerpts, *Theatre Arts*, 20 (September 1936): 679; "Fantastic Realism," *Directors on Directing*, ed. Toby Cole and Helen Krich Chinoy (Indianapolis: Bobbs-Merrill, 1953; rev. ed., 1963), 185-91.

25. Edwin Duerr, *The Length and Depth of Acting* (New York: Holt, Rinehart, and Winston, 1962), 474.

Chapter 2

1. Helen Deutsch and Stella Hanau, *The Provincetown* (New York: Farrar and Rinehart, Inc., 1931), 17.

2. Alice Lewisohn Crowley, *The Neighborhood Playhouse* (New York: Theatre Arts Books, 1959), 31.

3. Walter Prichard Eaton, *The Theatre Guild: The First Ten Years* (New York: Bretano, 1929), 6.

4. Nicholas A. Vardac, *Stage to Screen: Theatrical Method From Garrick to Griffith* (New York: Benjamin Blom, 1949; rpt., 1968), 59.

5. Lise-Lone Marker, *David Belasco: Naturalism in the American Theatre* (Princeton Univ. Press, 1975), 113.

6. Daniel Frohman, *Daniel Frohman Presents* (New York: Kendall and Sharp, 1935), 41.

7. An excellent source for examining early acting theories is found in Fred C. Blanchard, "Professional Theatre Schools in the Early Twentieth Century," in *History of Speech Education in America*, ed. Karl R. Wallace (New York: Appleton-Century-Crofts, Inc. , 1954), 617-40.

8. Charles Mackay, *Elementary Principles of Acting* (New York: Samuel French, 1934), xii.

9. Joseph Jefferson, *Rip Van Winkle: The Autobiography of Joseph Jefferson* (New York: Apple-Century-Crofts, n.d.), 336.

10. Richard Mansfield, "Concerning Acting," *The North American Theatre Review* (September 1894) : 337-40; also in Toby Cole and Helen Krich Chinoy, *Actors on Acting: The Theories, Techniques, and Practices of the Great Actors of all Times as Told in Their Own Words* (New York: Crown Publishers, 1949; 2d ed., 1954), 490-92.

11. William Gillette, *The Illusion of the First Time in Acting*, Papers on Acting, 1 (New York: Dramatic Museum of Columbia University, 1915; rpt., 1958).

12. Louis Calvert, *Problems of the Actor* (London: Simpkin, Marshall, Hamilton, Kent and Co., Ltd., 1918); An exellent comparison of early American acting theories with those of Stanislavski appears in Christine Edwards, *The Stanislavski Heritage: Its Contribution to the Russian and American Theatre* (New York: New York Univ. Press, 1965), 166-82.

13. Mrs. Minnie Maddern Fiske, *Mrs. Fiske, Her Views on Actors, Acting and the Problems of Production*, recorded by Alexander Woolcott (New York: The Century Co., 1917), 132.

14. Ibid., 89.

15. Constantin Stanislavski, *An Actor Prepares*, trans. Elizabeth Reynolds Hapgood (New York: Theatre Arts Books, 1936), 181.

16. William Winter, *The Life of David Belasco* (New York: Moffat Yard, 1918), 1: 109.

17. David Belasco, "Stage Realism of the Future," *Theatre Magazine* September 1913, 86.

18. David Belasco, "About Acting," *Saturday Evening Post*, 24 September 1921, 11, 94.

19. Ibid., 98.

20. David Belasco, "Why I Produce Unprofitable Plays," *Theatre Magazine*, March 1929, 21, 63.

21. Marker, *David Belasco*, 5, 202.

22. C. Stanislavsky: 1863-1963, 179-80; Morris Gest managed and supervised the M.A.T. tours in Europe and America from 1922 to 1924. He was also made an honorary member of the M.A.T.

23. Linda Arvidson (Mrs. D.W. Griffith), *When the Movies Were Young* (New York: E.P. Dutton, 1925), 223.

24. Vardac, *Stage to Screen*, 218.

25. Ibid., 250.

26. Lewis Jacobs, *The Rise of the American Film: A Critical History* (New York: Harcourt Brace and Co., 1939), 60.

27. Ibid., 61.

28.   Ibid., 87, quoting *The Moving Picture World*, 10 March 1910.

29.   John Drinkwater, *The Life and Times of Carl Laemmle* (New York: G.P. Putnam's Sons, 1931), 141.

30.   Frohman, *Daniel Frohman Presents*, 275.

31.   Arvidson, *When Movies Were Young*, 105.

32.   D. W. Griffith, "Pictures vs. One Night Stands," *Independent*, 88 (11 December 1916): 448.

33.   D. W. Griffith, "What I Demand of Movie Stars," *Motion Picture Classic*, February 1917, 68.

34.   D. W. Griffith, "A Poet Who Writes on Motion Picture Film," *The Theatre*, 19 (June 1914): 312.

35.   Mae Marsh, *Screen Acting* (Los Angeles: Photo-Star Publishing Co., 1921), 97.

36.   Griffith, "What I Demand of Movie Stars," 40.

37.   Ibid.

38.   *New York Dramatic Mirror*, 3 December 1913, 36.

39.   Jacobs, *Rise of American Film*, 203.

40.   Ibid., 217.

41.   Helen T. Broeck, "From Comedy to Tragedy: An Interview with John Barrymore," *Theatre Magazine*, July 1916, 23.

42.   Realistic acting in America was based upon European theories and controversies dating back to Denis Diderot's *The Paradox of Acting* (1830) and François Talma's "Reflections on Acting" (1877). Diderot believed an actor must portray emotions without actually feeling them; Talma felt the actor must feel true emotions as if they were his own. That basic conflict between physical and inner techniques permeates the history of twentieth century acting styles. Stanislavski's system has been interpreted along both lines from its inception in Moscow to its absorption in Hollywood.

43.   For more on the "Griffith Girls," *see* Anthony Slide, *The Griffith Actresses* (Cranbury, N.J.: A.S. Barnes and Co., 1973); For a complete list of Griffith films, *see* Robert M. Henderson, *D. W. Griffith: His Life and Work* (New York: Oxford Univ. Press, 1972), 293-309.

44.   Laurette Taylor, "The Quality You Need Most," *The Green Book Magazine*, April 1914, 556-62; also in Cole and Chinoy, *Actors on Acting*, 517-20.

45.   Reported by Shelley Winters in *Actors Talk About Acting: Fourteen Interviews with Stars of the Theatre*, ed. Lewis Funke and John E. Booth (New York: Random House, 1962), 314.

46.   Marsh, *Screen Acting*, 117.

47.   Ibid., 79.

48.   Klumph, *Screen Acting*, 29.

49.   Lillian Gish, *Lillian Gish: The Movies, Mr. Griffith and Me* (Englewood Cliffs, N.J.: Prentice Hall, 1969), 97-98, 192-93.

50.   Ibid., 97.

51.   Stanislavski, *An Actor Prepares*, 168.

52.   Gish, *Lillian Gish*, 84-85.

53. For a complete survey of sense-memory exercises utilized in later Method training, *see* Robert H. Hethmon, *Strasberg at the Actors Studio: Tape Recorded Sessions* (New York: The Viking Press, 1965), 96-104.

54. Gish, *Lillian Gish*, 85.

55. Constantin Stanislavski, "The Hard Job of Being an Actor" (1924), in *Stanislavski's Legacy*, 12.

56. Gish, *Lillian Gish*, 95-96.

57. Marsh, *Screen Acting*, 52.

58. Gish, *Lillian Gish*, 100.

59. Vardac, *Stage to Screen*, 218, quoting P. Whitney, "Expressing Movie Emotion," *Vanity Fair*, October 1919; Stanislavski himself did not consider melodrama as a cliché form of acting, but rather spoke of it as an artistic challenge to the imagination. *See* Stanislavski, "Why and When Play Melodrama," in *Stanislavski's Legacy*, 147.

60. These films are available through Blackhawk Films, The Eastin-Phalin Corp., Davenport, Iowa.

61. Charles Chaplin, "How I Made My Success," *Theatre Magazine*, September 1915, 121; also in Cole and Chinoy, *Actors on Acting*, 523.

62. *The New Encyclopaedia Britannica*, 15th ed., Macropaedia, s.v. "Acting," by Lee Strasberg.

63. Gish, *Lillian Gish*, 293.

64. Homer Croy, Starmaker: *The Story of D.W. Griffith* (New York: Duell, Sloan and Pearce, 1959), 178.

65. Arthur Knight, The Liveliest Art: *A Panoramic History of The Movies* (New York: The New American Library, Inc., 1957), 148.

66. Jacobs, *Rise of the American Film*, 457.

67. Croy, *Starmaker*, 176.

68. Richard Schickel, *The Men Who Made the Movies: Interviews* (New York: Atheneum, 1975), 68.

69. Ibid., 171.

70. Charles Higham, *The Art of the American Film* (New York: Doubleday and Co., 1973), 87.

Chapter 3

1. "Paul Orlenev and His Company of Russian Actors," *Theatre Magazine*, V, December 1905, p. xi; Cited by Clifford Ashby, "Alla Nazimova and the Advent of the New Acting in America," *Quarterly Journal of Speech*, XLV, 2 (April, 1959), p.182. Much of the information about Nazimova is derived from Ashby's highly informative article.

2. *New York Times*, 23 March 1905; Cited by Ashby, p. 184.

3. *New York Times*, 4 November 1906; Cited by Ashby, p. 184.

4. *New York Times*, 20 January 1907; cited by Ashby, 186.

5. *The New York Dramatic Mirror*, 26 January 1907, 3.

6. *Theatre Magazine*, 7 (March 1907): 72.

7. "Russian Artiste Becomes an American Star," *Theatre Magazine*, 7 (January 1907): 13.

8. Morton Eustis, *Players at Work: Acting According to the Actors* (New York: Theatre Arts Books, 1937), 85.

9. Ashby, "Alla Nazimova," 188.

10. Christine Edwards, *The Stanislavsky Heritage* (New York: New York Univ. Press, 1965), 215.

11. J. Rankin Towse, *New York Evening Post,* 30 January, 1923.

12. Stark Young, *Glamour* (New York: Charles Scribner's Sons, 1925), 47.

13. Kenneth MacGowan, "And Again Repertory: The Moscow Art Theatre and Shakespeare Divide New York Honors," *Theatre Arts Monthly*, 7, No.2 (April 1923): 89-90.

14. Ludwig Lewisohn, "An American Art Theatre—Why Not?" *Theatre Magazine*, August 1923, 9.

15. David Garfield, *A Player's Place: The Story of the Actors Studio* (New York: Macmillan Publishing Co., 1980), 8-9.

16. Magarshack, *Stanislavski, A Life*, 364.

17. Robert Albert Johnston, "The Moscow Art Theatre in America" (Ph.D. diss., Northwestern, 1951); cited in Edwards, *The Stanislavsky Heritage*, 233.

18. Belasco, "Why I Produce Unprofitable Plays," 21.

19. The teaching activities of individual M.A.T. members are fully discussed in Edwards, *The Stanislavsky Heritage*, 239-45.

20. Richard Boleslavski, "Stanislavski—The Man and His Methods," *Theatre Magazine*, 37 (April 1923): 27, 74, 80.

21. Ibid., 27.

22. Richard Boleslavski, "The Laboratory Theatre," *Theatre Arts Monthly*, 7 (July 1923): 245.

23. Ronald A. Willis, "The American Lab Theatre," *Tulane Drama Review*, 9, No. 1 (Fall 1964): 112-13.

24. Michael C. Hardy, "The Theatre of Richard Boleslavsky" (Ph.D. diss., Michigan, 1971), p.77. Much of the following is derived from this informative work.

25. Ibid., 102.

26. Richard Boleslavski, "The Creative Theatre" (1923), trans. Michael Barron, First Executive Secretary of the American Laboratory Theatre. The typescript MS is housed in the Theatre Collection of the New York Public Library.

27. Hardy, "Richard Boleslavsky," 84.

28. Hethmon, *Strasberg at the Actors Studio*, 145.

29. Hardy, "Richard Boleslavsky," 119.

30. Ibid. *See* also Francis Fergusson, "The Notion of 'Action'," *Tulane Drama Review*, 9, No.1 (Fall 1964): 85-87.

31. Stella Adler, "The Actor in the Group Theatre," in *Actors on Acting*, Cole and Chinoy, 538.

32.   Harold Clurman, *The Fervent Years: The Story of the Group Theatre and the Thirties* (New York: Hill and Wang, 1945), 41.

33.   Gordon Rogoff, "Lee Strasberg: Burning Ice," *Tulane Drama Review*, 9, No. 2 (Winter 1964): 145-46.

34.   Stella Adler, "The Reality of Doing," *Tulane Drama Review*, 9, No. 1 (Fall 1964): 139.

35.   Paul Gray, "Stanislavski and America: A Critical Chronology," 34.

36.   Adler, "The Actor in the Group Theatre," 539.

37.   Clurman, *The Fervent Years*, 130.

38.   Gray, "Stanislavski in America," 35.

39.   Ibid.

40.   "Three Meetings [With Stanislavski]," in Boris Filippov, *Actors Without Make-up* (Moscow: Progress Publishers, 1977), 59.

41.   Stanislavski's meeting with Adler is discussed in Garfield, *A Player's Place*, 34.

42.   Ibid, 32.

43.   Ibid.

Chapter 4

1.   Arthur Knight, *The Liveliest Art* (New York: The New American Library, Inc., 1957), 161. For more on films in the thirties, *see* John Baxter, *Hollywood in the Thirties* (New York: A.S. Barnes, 1968).

2.   Richard Schickel, *The Men Who Made the Movies* (New York: Atheneum, 1975), 42.

3.   Ibid.

4.   Paul Muni, "The Mechanics of Movie Acting," in *Actors on Acting*, ed. Cole and Chinoy, 530.

5.   Hardy, "Richard Boleslavsky," 56.

6.   "Richard Boleslavsky," *Motion Picture Magazine*, 53 (March 1937): 33.

7.   Russell Janney, "Richard Boleslawski,"[sic] *New York Herald Tribune*, 31 January 1937.

8.   Hardy, "Richard Boleslavsky," 112.

9.   Francis Fergusson, "The Notion of 'Action'," 8.

10.   *See* Baxter, *Hollywood in the Thirties*, 3.

11.   Hardy, "Richard Boleslavsky," 130.

12.   Review of *Garden of Allah* (1936) with Marlene Dietrich and Charles Boyer, *Daily Variety* 31 October 1936, 3.

13.   Review of *The Last of Mrs. Cheney* (1937) with Joan Crawford, William Powell, and Robert Montgomery, *The Hollywood Reporter*, 15 February 1937, 3.

14.   *See*, for example, *Newsweek*, 21 November 1936, 20; *Film Daily*, 3 November 1936, 6; *Box Office*, 14 November 1936, 51.

15. William Boehnel, *New York World Telegram*, 24 September 1936, 28.

16. *New Theatre Magazine*, November 1936, 34.

17. The West Coast acting school is discussed in Ouspenskaya's obituary, *New York Times*, 4 December 1949, 108. For more on Ouspenskaya's teaching method, *see* Garfield, *A Player's Place*, 11-13.

18. Harold Clurman, *The Fervent Years*, 159.

19. Michael Ciment, *Kazan on Kazan* (New York: Viking Press, 1973), 19.

20. Ibid., 24.

21. *Who's Who in the Theatre* (New York: Pitman Publishing, 1972), 15th ed., 443.

22. Harold Clurman, *All People Are Famous* (New York: Harcourt, Brace, Jovanovich, 1974), 119.

23. John Garfield, *A Player's Place*, 78, 274.

24. Knight, *The Liveliest Art*, 246.

Chapter 5

1. Ciment, *Kazan on Kazan*, 36.

2. Robert Lewis, *Method or Madness?* (New York: Samuel French, 1958), 15.

3. Ciment, *Kazan on Kazan*, 37.

4. Gray, "Stanislavski and America: A Critical Chronology," 43.

5. Ibid., 45.

6. Rogoff, "Lee Strasberg: Burning Ice," 136.

7. Strasberg discussed the derivation of the term *The Method,* implying that "outsiders" were in effect responsible for distinguishing the particular method of the Actors Studio, whereas Studio members simply referred to "Stanislavski's ideas" or "Stanislavski's method." *See* Robert H. Hethmon, *Strasberg at the Actors Studio,* 41.

8. Lee Strasberg, "Affective Memory," a lecture given at the Lee Strasberg Theatre Institute, Los Angeles, California, July 1973.

9. Joan Barthel, "The Master of the Method Plays a Role Himself," *New York Times*, 2 February 1975, Sect. 2, p.1.

10. Stanislavski, "Types of Actors," in *Stanislavski's Legacy*, 14.

11. Lee Strasberg, "Working with Live Material," *Tulane Drama Review*, 9, No.1 (Fall, 1964): 132.

12. Strasberg has acknowledged Vakhtangov's influence. *See*, for example, Hethmon, *Strasberg at the Actors Studio*, 308-89.

13. Stanislavski, "The Art of the Actor and the Director," in *Stanislavski's Legacy*, 178.

14. Stella Adler, "The Reality of Doing," *Tulane Drama Review*, 9, No. 1 (Fall 1964): 143.

15. Vera Soloviova, "Reality of Doing," *Tulane Drama Review*, 9, No. 1 (Fall 1964): 142.

16. Sanford Meisner, "Reality of Doing," *Tulane Drama Review*, 9, No. 1 (Fall 1964): 144.

17.   For more on Strasberg and the private moment *see* David Garfield, *A Player's Place*, 172-74. A highly unsettling criticism of Strasberg's work appears in Gordon Rogoff's "Lee Strasberg: Burning Ice"; for Lee Strasberg's belated response, *see* "Strasberg vs. TDR," *Tulane Drama Review*, 11, No. 1 (Fall 1966): 234-39. For more on Strasberg as a teacher, see Jean Scharfenberg, "Lee Strasberg: Teacher" (Ph.D. diss, Wisconsin, 1963).

18.   Lee Strasberg, "Private Moments," a lecture given at the Lee Strasberg Theatre Institute, Los Angeles, California, 23 July 1973.

19.   Strasberg, "Working with Live Material," 123.

20.   Meisner, "Reality of Doing," 148.

21.   Ibid., 40 n. Strasberg himself did not want to undergo analysis, although he did recommend it for others. *See* David Garfield, *A Player's Place*, 147.

22.   Meisner, "Reality of Doing," p. 150.

23.   Harold Clurman, "There's a Method in British Acting," *New York Times*, January 12, 1964, Sec. 2, p.62.

24.   Boleslavski, "Stanislavski—The Man and His Methods," p. 80.

25.   The M.A.T. seminars are discussed in David Garfield, *A Player's Place*, 177.

26.   In the 1960s, Strasberg conceded that physical training has a place in the craft of acting. He was influenced by a Montreal performance of the Peking State Opera, and tried to incorporate Chinese physical training into the Actors Studio (specifically Tao Chi Chian). Ibid., 197.

27.   Ibid., 73. David Garfield offers an informative discussion of the early Actors Studio experiments in cable TV drama.

28.   Ibid., pp. 212-213.

29.   David Garfield offers a lengthy and informative discussion of the unsuccessful efforts of the Actors Studio Theatre and the artistic management of Lee Strasberg. Ibid., 214-47.

30.   Ibid., 245; Critical reviews of the productions are quoted in Garfield's account of the Actors Studio Theatre presentations.

31.   *See*, for example, Vincent Canby's review of *Three Sisters*, *New York Times* 30 June 1977, Drama section, 1.

Chapter 6

1.   Oscar Brockett and Robert Findlay, *Century of Innovation* (Englewood Cliffs, N.J.: Prentice Hall, 1971), 573.

2.   Brooks Atkinson, *Broadway* (New York: Macmillan, 1970; rev., 1974), 407.

3.   Walter Kerr, *Pieces at Eight* (New York: Simon and Schuster, 1957), 237.

4.   Brockett and Findlay, *Century of Innovation*, 755. For more on Chaiken and the Open Theatre, *see* Robert Pasolli, *A Book on the Open Theatre* (Indianapolis: The Bobbs-Merrill Co., 1970)

5.   Jerzy Grotowski, *Towards a Poor Theatre* (New York: Simon and Schuster, 1968), 15-16.

6.   Ibid., 19.

7.   Brockett and Findlay, *Century of Innovation*, 703.

8.   Gerald Mast, *A Short History of the Movies* (Chicago: Univ. of Chicago Press, 3d ed., 1981), 268.

9.   Ibid., 269. The official fight against the Breen Code began with Otto Preminger's *Moon is Blue* (1953) which was released without Code approval. The attendant publicity assured box office success, and the code fought a losing battle for survival until its demise in 1968.

10.   Cobbett Steinberg, *Reel Facts,* pp. 259-261.

11.   Gordon Gow, *Hollywood in the Fifties* (New York: A.S. Barnes and Co., 1971), 119-20.

12.   Ciment, *Kazan on Kazan*, 71-72.

13.   Ibid., 52.

14.   Ibid., 40.

15.   Ibid., 40-41.

16.   Robert Lewis, "Would You Please Talk to Those People," *Tulane Drama Review*, 9, No.2 (Winter 1964): 99.

17.   Edwards, *The Stanislavsky Heritage*, p.278; from a letter written to Elizabeth Reynolds Hapgood on 14 January 1959.

18.   David Garfield, *A Player's Place*, 94-95.

19.   Thomas R. Atkins, *Sexuality in the Movies* (Bloomington: Indiana Univ. Press, 1975), 114.

20.   Funke and Booth, eds., *Actors Talk About Acting*, 215.

21.   Robert Ward, "Rod Steiger, Hollywood's Last Angry Man," *American Film*, February 1982, 39.

22.   Thomas W. Bohn and Richard Stromgren, *Light and Shadows: A History of Motion Pictures* (New York: Alfred Publishers, 1975), 412.

23.   Cobbett Steinberg, *Reel Facts*, 2d ed., (New York: Random House, Vintage Books, 1982), 42-43.

24.   Bohn and Stromgren, *Light and Shadows*, 453.

25.   Ibid., 452-55.

26.   Ibid., 408.

27.   Ibid., 458.

28.   Probst, *Off Camera*, 61; "Dialogue on Film: Dustin Hoffman," *American Film*, April 1983, 26-28, 69-70.

29.   "Dialogue on Film: Dustin Hoffman," 70.

30.   Ibid.

31.   Ibid.

32.   Ciment, *Kazan on Kazan*, 43; Kazan also discusses his work with actors in *Directors at Work*, eds. Bernard R. Kantor, Irwin R. Blacker, and Anne Kramer (New York: Funk and Wagnalls, 1975), 168.

Chapter 7

1. *Variety*, 15 February 1984, "Film Costs Will Soar 36% in 1984," 1, 38. According to industry statistics, 142 films were produced in 1984, compared to 127 films in 1983, and 116 films in 1982.

2. *Variety*, 29 August 1979, 12. Some of the highest-grossing films of that period included *The Godfather*, *Jaws*, *Star Wars*, *Close Encounters of the Third Kind*, *Superman*, and the low-budget nostalgia film, *American Graffiti*.

3. Review of *Heaven's Gate*, *Variety*, 26 November 1978.

4. Gerald Mast, *A Short History of the Movies*, 448.

5. Review of *Coming Home*, *Variety* 17 February 1978.

6. *See*, for example, Michael Kernan, "Fathering of a Hit: Kramer vs. Corman," *Washington Post*, 29 December 1979, Sec. C, p.1.

7. Review of *On Golden Pond*, *Variety*, 17 September 1980.

8. A list of Emmy Award nominees and winners from the Actors Studio is available from the Actors Studio, New York. It should be noted that dates are sometimes at odds with other primary sources. The Studio listings can be verified against information from the Academy of Television Arts and Sciences, Los Angeles, or from works such as *Variety International Showbusiness Reference*, Garland Publishing, New York and London.

9. The formation of the Actors Studio West is fully discussed by David Garfield, *A Player's Place*, 256-62.

10. Interview, 13 February 1984.

11. Hethmon, *Strasberg at the Actors Studio*, 20.

12. *See* "The Actors Studio Membership List, 1984," available from the Actors Studio in New York. Dates of membership for Studio actors nominated for Academy Awards are listed in Appendix B.

13. José Ferrer in *Actors Talk About Acting*, 125.

14. Leonard Probst, ed., *Off Camera*, New York: Stein and Day, 1975, p.95; Dustin Hoffman went on to win five Academy Award nominations for Best Actor in ensuing years (see Appendix B).

15. Hethmon, *Strasberg at the Actors Studio*, p. 20.

16. Lynde McCormick, "Robert Duvall," *American Film*, September, 1981, 42.

17. Probst, *Off Camera*, 61.

18. Ibid., 103-6; "Dialogue on Film: Dustin Hoffman," *American Film*, April, 1983, 70.

19. *Actors Talk About Acting*, 377.

20. Ibid., 171.

21. Michael Bygrave and Joan Goodman, "Jane Fonda: Banking on Message Movies," *American Film*, November, 1981, 40.

22. *Actors Talk About Acting*, 314.

23. Sondra Lowell, "About Those Strasberg Tapes," *Los Angeles Times*, 12 November 1983, Part 5, 1, 6.

24. Review of *Raging Bull, Wall Street Journal*, 28 November, 1980, 40.

25. "Dialogue on Film: Robert DeNiro," *American Film*, March 1981, 47.

26. Ibid., 40.

27. Mel Gussow, "Dustin Hoffman's *Salesman*," *New York Times Magazine*, 18 March 1984, 37. This review examines Hoffman's re-entry in theatre as Willy Loman in Arthur Miller's contemporary classic, *Death of a Salesman* (1984).

28. Ibid., 86.

29. "Dialogue on Film: Dustin Hoffman," *American Film*, April, 1983, 27.

30. Ibid., 28.

31. Ibid., 27.

32. Ibid., 71.

33. Mike Bygrave and Joan Goodman, "Jane Fonda: Banking on Message Movies," *American Film*, November, 1981, 40.

34. Ibid., p. 40.

35. "20/20" feature segment on Paul Newman and Joanne Woodward, ABC TV, 29 March 1984.

36. Ibid.

37. Ibid.

38. Ibid.

39. Ibid.

40. Interview, 13 February 1984.

41. "Dialogue on Film: Robert DeNiro," *American Film*, March, 1981, 40.

42. "Dialogue on Film: Dustin Hoffman," *American Film*, 70.

43. David Garfield, *A Player's Place*, 275.

Bibliography

Books

Agnew, Frances. *Motion Picture Acting.* New York, 1913.

Alpers, B. *The Theatre of the Social Mask.* Translated by Mark Schmidt. New York: The Group Theatre, 1934.

Anderson, John, and Rene Fulop-Miller. *The American Theatre and the Motion Picture in America.* New York: Dial Press, 1938.

Artaud, Antonin. *The Theatre and its Double.* Translated by Mary Caroline Richards. New York: Grove Press, 1958.

Arvidson, Linda [Mrs. D.W. Griffith]. *When the Movies Were Young.* New York: E.P. Dutton and Co., 1925.

Atkins, Thomas R. *Sexuality in the Movies.* Bloomington: Indiana Univ. Press, 1975.

Atkinson, Brooks. *Broadway.* New York: Macmillan Co., 1970; rev. 1974.

Baer, D. Richard, ed. *The Film Buff's Bible of Motion Pictures (1915-1972).* Hollywood: Hollywood Film Archive, 1972.

Barrymore, John. *Confessions of an Actor.* Indianapolis: Bobbs-Merrill Co., 1926.

Baxter, John. *Hollywood in the Sixties.* New York: A.S. Barnes, 1972.

_____. *Hollywood in the Thirties.* New York: A.S. Barnes, 1968.

Belasco, David. *The Theatre Through Its Stage Door.* Edited by Louis V. Defoe, New York: Harper, 1919.

Boleslavski, Richard. *Acting: The First Six Lessons.* New York: Theatre Arts Books, 1949; Reprint, 1962.

Boucicault, Dion. *The Art of Acting.* Papers on Acting, 5th Series, No. 1. New York: Dramatic Museum of Columbia University, 1926.

Brecht, Bertolt. *Brecht on Theatre.* Translated by John Willet. New York: Hill and Wang, 1964.

Brockett, Oscar, and Robert Findlay. *Century of Innovation: A History of Theatre and Drama, 1870-1970.* Englewood Cliffs, N.J.: Prentice Hall, 1971.

Calvert, Louis, *Problems of the Actor,* London: Simpkin, Marshall, Hamilton, Kent and Co., 1918.

Chekhov, Michael. *To the Actor: On the Technique of Acting.* New York: Harper and Brothers, 1953.

Ciment, Michel. *Kazan on Kazan.* New York: Viking Press, 1973.

Clurman, Harold. *All People Are Famous.* New York: Harcourt, Brace, Jovanovich, 1974.

_____. *The Fervent Years: The Story of the Group Theatre and The Thirties.* New York: Hill and Wang, 1945; rev., 1957.

Cole, Toby, ed. *Acting: A Handbook of the Stanislavski Method.* New York: Crown Publishers, 1963.

_____, and Helen K. Chinoy, eds. *Actors on Acting: The Theories, Techniques, and Practices of the Great Actors of All Times as Told in Their Own Words*. New York: Crown Publishers, 1949; 2d ed., 1954.

_____. *Directors on Directing: A Source Book of the Modern Theatre*. New York: Bobbs-Merrill Co., 1953; rev., 1963.

Cooke, Alistair. *Douglas Fairbanks: The Making of a Screen Character*. New York: Museum of Modern Art, 1940.

Crowley, Alice Lewisohn. *The Neighborhood Playhouse: Leaves From a Theatre Scrapbook*. New York: Theatre Arts Books, 1959.

Crowther, Bosley, *The Lion's Share*. New York: E. P. Dutton and Co., 1957.

Croy, Homer, *Starmaker: The Story of D. W. Griffith*. New York: Duell, Sloan, and Pearce, 1959.

Darwin, Charles, *The Expression of the Emotions in Man and Animals*. London: J. Murray, 1872.

Deutsch, Helen and Stella Hanau, *The Provincetown*. New York: Farrar and Rinehart, 1931.

Diderot, Denis. "The Paradox of Acting," in William Archer, *Masks or Faces*. New York: Hill and Wang, 1957.

Drinkwater, John. *The Life and Adventures of Carl Laemmle*. New York: G.P. Putnam's Sons, 1931.

Duerr, Edwin. *The Length and Depth of Acting*. New York: Holt, Rinehart, and Winston, 1962.

Easty, Edward. *On Method Acting*. New York: House of Collectibles, 1966.

Eaton, Walter Prichard. *The Theatre Guild: The First Ten Years*. New York: Brentano, 1929.

Edwards, Christine. *The Stanislavsky Heritage: Its Contribution to the Russian and American Theatre*. New York: New York Univ. Press, 1965.

Eustis, Morton. *Players at Work: Acting According to the Actors*. New York: Theatre Arts Books, 1937.

Everson, William K. *American Silent Film*. New York. Oxford Univ. Press, 1978.

Filippov, Boris. *Actors Without Make-Up*. Moscow: Progress Publishers, 1977.

Fiske, Mrs. Minnie Maddern. *Mrs. Fiske, Her Views on Actors, Acting, and the Problems of Production*. Recorded by Alexander Woolcott. New York: The Century Co., 1917.

Frohman, Daniel. *Daniel Frohman Presents: An Autobiography*. New York: Kendall and Sharp, 1935.

_____. *Encore*. New York: Lee Furman, Inc., 1937.

Funke, Lewis, and John E. Booth. *Actors Talk About Acting: Fourteen Interviews With Stars of the Theatre*. New York: Random House, 1962.

Garfield, David. *A Player's Place: The Story of the Actors Studio*. New York: Macmillan Co., 1980.

Gassner, John. *Dramatic Soundings: Evaluations and Retractions Culled from 30 Years of Dramatic Criticism*. New York: Crown Publishers, 1968.

Geduld, Harry M. *The Birth of the Talkies*. Bloomington: Indiana Univ. Press, 1975.

_____. *Focus on D. W. Griffith*. Englewood Cliffs, N.J.: Prentice Hall, 1971.

Gillette, William H. *The Illusion of the First Time in Acting*. Papers on Acting, No. 1. New York: Dramatic Museum of Columbia University, 1915, Reprint, 1958.

Gish, Lillian (With Ann Pinchot). *Lillian Gish: The Movies, Mr. Griffith and Me*. Englewood Cliffs, N.J.: Prentice Hall, 1969.

Gorchakov, Nikolai. *Stanislavski Directs*. New York: Universal Library, 1962.

_____. *The Theatre in Soviet Russia*. Translated by Edgar Lehrman. New York: Columbia Univ. Press, 1957.

_____. *The Vakhtangov School of Stage Art*. New York: Theatre Arts, 1961.

Gow, Gordon. *Hollywood in the Fifties*. New York: A.S. Barnes, 1971.

Grotowski, Jerzy. *Towards a Poor Theatre*. New York: Simon and Schuster, 1968.

Grube, Max. *The Story of the Meiningen*. Translated by Anne Marie Koller. Coral Gables: Univ. of Miami Press, 1963.

Hagen, Uta. *Respect for Acting*. New York: Macmillan Co., 1973.

Hammerton, J.A., ed. *The Actor's Art: Theatrical Reminiscences, Methods of Study and Advice to Aspirants Specially Contributed by Leading Actors of the Day*. London: George Redway, 1897.

Henderson, Robert M. *D.W. Griffith: His Life and Work*. New York: Oxford Univ. Press, 1972.

Hethmon, Robert H., ed. *Strasberg at the Actors Studio: Tape Recorded Sessions*. New York: Viking Press, 1965.

Hewitt, Barnard. *Theatre U.S.A.: 1668-1957*. New York: McGraw Hill, 1959.

Higham, Charles. *The Art of the American Film: 1900-1971*. New York: Doubleday and Co., 1973.

_____, and Joel Greenberg. *Hollywood in the Forties*. New York: A.S. Barnes, 1968.

Hornblow, Arthur. *A History of American Theatre*. 2 Vols. Philadelphia: J.B. Lippincott Co., 1919.

_____. *Training for the Stage: Some Hints for Those About to Choose the Player's Career, With a Foreword by Mr. David Belasco*. Philadelphia and London: J.B. Lippincott Co., 1916.

Hughes, Elinor. *Famous Stars of Filmdom*. Boston, 1931.

Hughes, Glenn. *A History of the American Theatre, 1700-1950*. New York: Samuel French, 1951.

Jacobs, Lewis. *The Rise of the American Film: A Critical History*. New York: Harcourt Brace and Co., 1939.

Jefferson, Joseph. *Rip Van Winkle: The Autobiography of Joseph Jefferson*. New York: Appleton Century Crofts, n.d.

Kantor, Bernard R., Irwin R. Blacker and Anne Kramer, eds. *Directors at Work: Interviews With American Filmakers*. New York: Funk and Wagnalls, 1975.

Kerr, Walter, *Pieces at Eight*. New York: Simon and Schuster, 1957.

_____. *The Silent Clowns*. New York: Knopf, 1975.

Klumph, Inez and Helen. *Screen Acting: Its Requirements and Rewards*. New York: Falk Publishing Co., 1922.

Knight, Arthur. *The Liveliest Art: A Panoramic History of the Movies*. New York: New American Library, 1957.

Kolker, Robert Phillip. *A Cinema of Loneliness: Penn, Kubrick, Coppola, Scorsese, Altman*. New York: Oxford Univ. Press, 1980.

Koszarski, Richard. *Hollywood Directors: 1914-1940*. New York: Oxford Univ. Press, 1976.

Kracauer, Siegfried. *Theory of Film*. New York: 1960.

Kristi, G.W. *Stanislavski's Complete Works*. 8 Vols. Berlin: Hensscherverlag, 1955.

Lewes, George Henry. *On Actors and the Art of Acting*. New York: Grove Press, 1957.

Lewis, Robert. *Advice to the Players*. New York: Harper and Row, 1980.

_____. *Method or Madness?* New York: Samuel French, 1958.

Lindsay, Vachel. *The Art of the Moving Picture*. New York: 1915.

Mackay, Charles. *Elementary Principles of Acting*. New York: Samuel French, 1934.

Mackay, F.F. *The Art of Acting*. New York: F.F. Mackay, 1913.

Magarshack, David. *Stanislavski, A Life*. New York: Chanticleer Press, 1951.

_____. trans. *Stanislavski on the Art of the Stage*. London: Faber and Faber, 1950.

Marker, Lise-Lone. *David Belasco: Naturalism in the American Theatre*. Princeton: Princeton Univ. Press, 1975.

Marsh, Mae. *Screen Acting*. Los Angeles: Photo-Star Publishing Co., 1922.

Mast, Gerald. *A Short History of the Movies*. Chicago: Univ. of Chicago Press, 3d ed., 1981.

_____. *The Comic Mind: Comedy and the Movies*. Chicago: Univ. of Chicago Press, 2d ed., 1981.

Matthews, Brader. *On Acting*. New York: Scribner's, 1914.

_____. ed. *Papers on Acting*. New York: Hill and Wang, 1958.

McDonald, Donald. *Stage and Screen: Interviews with Walter Kerr, New York Herald-Tribune, and Stanley Kramer, Film Producer and Director, With a Comment by Edward Reed*. Santa Barbara: Center for the Study of Democratic Institutions, 1962.

Moore, Sonia, *The Stanislavski System: The Professional Training of an Actor.* New York: Viking Press, 1960; Reprint, 1965; 3d ed., 1974.

Motion Picture Review Digest. New York: H.W. Wilson Co., Vol. s, No. 52, 1937.

Naumberg, Nancy, ed. *We Make the Movies.* New York: W.W. Norton and Co., 1937.

Nemirovitch-Dantchenko, Vladimar. *My Life in the Russian Theatre.* Translated by John Cournos. Boston: Little, Brown and Co., 1936.

New York Times Directory of the Film. New York: Random House, Arno Press, 1971.

Nicoll, Allardyce. *Film and Theatre.* New York: Thomas Y. Crowell Co., 1936; Reprint, 1937.

O'Dell, Paul (with Anthony Slide). *D. W. Griffith and the Rise of Hollywood.* New York: Barnes, 1971.

Paramount Picture School Catalogue. New York: Paramount Pictures, 1925.

Parish, James Robert, and William T. Leonard. *Hollywood Players: The Thirties.* New York: Arlington House, 1976.

Parish, James Robert, and Michael R. Pitts. *Film Directors: A Guide to Their American Films.* Metuchen, N.J.: Scarecrow Press, 1974.

Pasolli, Robert. *A Book on the Open Theatre.* Indianapolis: Bobbs-Merrill Co., 1970.

Pickford, Mary, et al. *Cinema: Practical Courses in Cinema Acting in Ten Complete Lessons.* London: Standard Art Book Co., n.d.

Platt, Agnes. *Practical Hints on Acting for the Cinema.* New York: E.P. Dutton and Co., 1923.

Probst, Leonard, ed. *Off Camera: Leveling About Themselves—Al Pacino, Paul Newman, Diana Rigg, George C. Scott, Dustin Hoffman, Mike Nichols, Elaine May, Barbara Walters, Edwin Newman, Lynn Redgrave, Dick Cavett, Marlo Thomas, Zero Mostel, Shirley MacLaine, Angela Lansbury, Gwen Verdon, Woody Allen.* New York: Stein and Day, 1975.

Pudovkin, V.I. *Film Technique and Film Acting: The Cinema Writings of V.I. Pudovkin.* Translated by Ivor Montagu. London: Vision Press, 1954.

Ramsaye, Terry. *A Million and One Nights: A History of the Motion Pictures.* 2 Vols. New York: 1926.

Ribot, Théodule. *Psychology of the Emotions.* New York: 1897.

Ross, Lillian and Helen. *The Player.* New York: Simon and Schuster, 1962.

Rotha, Paul. *The Film Till Now.* New York: Funk and Wagnalls, 1949.

Scheuing, F.M. *Motion Picture Acting.* New York: 1913.

Schickel, Richard. *The Men Who Made the Movies: Interviews with Frank Capra, George Cukor, Howard Hawks, Alfred Hitchcock, Vincente Minelli, King Vidor, Raoul Walsh, and William a. Wellman.* New York: Atheneum, 1975.

Shelley, Frank. *Stage to Screen.* London: Pendulum, 1947.

Simonov, Ruben. *Stanislavsky's Protegé: Eugene Vakhtangov.* Translated and adapted by Miriam Goldina. New York: Drama Book Specialists, 1969.

Skinner, Otis. *Footlights and Spotlights: Recollections of My Life on the Stage.* Indianapolis: Bobbs-Merrill Co., 1924.

Slide, Anthony. *The Griffith Actresses.* Cranbury, N.J.: A.S. Barnes and Co., 1973.

Stanislavski, Constantin. *An Actor Prepares.* Translated by Elizabeth Reynolds Hapgood. New York: Theatre Arts Books, 1936.

———. *Building a Character.* Translated by Elizabeth Reynolds Hapgood. New York: Theatre Arts Books, 1949.

———. *Creating a Role.* Translated by Elizabeth Reynolds Hapgood. New York: Theatre Arts Books, 1961.

———. *My Life in Art.* 2d ed. Translated by J.J. Robbins. New York: Theatre Arts Books, 1924; Reprint, 1948.

———. *K. Stanislavsky: 1863-1963, Man and Actor, Stanislavsky and the World Theatre, Stanislavsky's Letters.* Translated by Vic Schneierson. Moscow: Progress Publishers, n.d. [ca. 1964].

_____. *Stanislavski's Legacy: A Collection of Comments on a Variety of Aspects of an Actor's Art and Life.* Edited and translated by Elizabeth Reynolds Hapgood. New York: Theatre Arts Books, 1958.

Stanislavski Today: Commentaries on K.S. Stanislavski. New York: American Center for Stanislavski Theatre Art, 1973.

Stearns, Harold. *The Stage and the Movies in America, A Reappraisal.* New York: Hillman-Curl, 1937.

Steinberg, Cobbett. *Reel Facts.* 2d ed., New York: Random House, Vintage Books, 1982.

Symons, James M. *Meyerhold's Theatre of the Grotesque: The Post-Revolutionary Productions, 1920-1932.* Coral Gables: Univ. of Miami Press, 1971.

Truitt, Evelyn Mack. *Who Was Who on Screen.* New York: R.R. Bowker Co., 1974.

Vardac, A. Nicholas. *Stage to Screen: Theatrical Method From Garrick to Griffith.* New York and London: Benjamin Blom, 1949, Reprint, 1968.

Variety International Showbusiness Reference. New York and London: Garland Publishing, 1981.

Walker, Alexander. *Stardom: The Hollywood Phenomenon.* New York: Stein and Day, 1970.

Watts, Stephen, ed. *Behind the Screen: How Films are Made.* New York: Dodge Publishing Co., 1938.

Articles

Adler, Stella. "The Actor in the Group Theatre" In *Actors on Acting.* Edited by Toby Cole and Helen K. Chinoy, 536-40. New York: Crown Publishers, 1949; 2d ed. 1954.

_____. "The Reality of Doing." *Tulane Drama Review,* 9, No"1 (Fall 1964): 136-55.

Ashby, Clifford. "Alla Nazimova and the Advent of the New Acting in America." *Quarterly Journal of Speech,* 45, No. 2 (April 1959): 182-88.

Barrymore, Lionel. "The Actor." In *Behind the Screen: How Films Are Made.* Edited by Stephen Watts. London: Arthur Baker, 1938.

Barthel, Joan. "The Master of the Method Plays a Role Himself." *New York Times,* 2 February 1975, sec. 2, p. 1.

Belasco, David. "About Acting." *Saturday Evening Post,* 24 September 1921.

_____. "David Belasco Attacks Stage Tradition." *Theatre Magazine,* May, 1911, 164-68.

_____. "Stage Realism of the Future." *Theatre Magazine,* 1913, 86.

_____. "Why I Produce Unprofitable Plays." *Theatre Magazine,* March 1929.

Bentley, Eric. "Are Stanislavski and Brecht Commensurable?" *Tulane Drama Review,* 9, No. 1 (Fall 1964): 69-76.

Blanchard, Fred C. "Professional Theatre Schools in the Early Twentieth Century." In *History of Speech Education in America.* Edited by Karl R. Wallace, 617-40. New York: Appleton Century Crofts, 1954.

"Boleslavski." *Motion Picture Magazine,* 53 (March 1937) 20.

Boleslavski, Richard. "The First Lesson in Acting: A Pseudo-Morality." *Theatre Arts Magazine,* 7, No. 4 (October 1923): 284-92.

_____. "The Laboratory Theatre." *Theatre Arts Monthly,* 7 (July 1923): 244-50.

_____. "Stanislavsky—The Man and His Methods." *Theatre Magazine,* 37 (April 1923).

Box Office, November 14, 1936, p. 51.

Brecht, Bertolt. "A New Technique of Acting." Translated by Eric Bentley. *Theatre Arts,* 33 (January 1949): 38-40.

_____. "Notes on Stanislavski." Translated by Carl R. Mueller. *Tulane Drama Review,* 9, No. 2 (Winter 1964): 155-66.

Brady, Alice. "The Problem of Casting by Type." *Theatre,* 50 (December 1929).

Broeck, Helen T. "From Comedy to Tragedy: An Interview with John Barrymore." *Theatre Magazine,* July 1916, 23.

Bush, W. Stephen. "Belasco on Motion Pictures." *The Moving Picture World,* 13 June 1914.

Bygrave, Mike and Goodman, Joan. "Jane Fonda: Banking on Message Movies", *American Film,* November 1981, 40.

Carr, Harry C. "How Griffith Picks His Leading Women." *Photoplay,* December 1918, 24-26.

Chaiken, Joseph. "The Open Theatre." *Tulane Drama Review,* 9, No. 2 (Winter 1964): 191-97.

Chaplin, Charles. "How I Made My Success." *Theatre Magazine,* September 1915.

Clurman, Harold. "There's a Method in British Acting." *New York Times,* 12 January 1964, sec. 6, p. 62.

Coger, Leslie Irene. "Stanislavski Changes His Mind." *Tulane Drama Review,* 9, No. 1 (Fall 1964): 63-68.

Cowl, Jane. "Is Stage Emotion Real?" *Theatre,* 23 (March 1916).

Davis, Bette. "On Acting in Films." *Theatre Arts,* 25 (September 1941): 633-39.

————. "The Actress Plays Her Part." *We Make the Movies.* Edited by Nancy Naumberg. New York: W.W. Norton, 1937.

"Dialogue on Film: Dustin Hoffman," *American Film,* April 1983.

"Dialogue on Film: Robert De Niro," *American Film,* March 1981: 39-47.

Eisenstein, Sergei. "Doing Without Actors." *Cinema,* June 1930.

————. "Filmic Art and Training." *Close Up,* March 1930.

————. "Through Theatre to Cinema." *Theatre Arts Monthly,* September 1936.

Fergusson, Francis. "The Notion of 'Action.'" *Tulane Drama Review,* 9, No. 1 (Fall 1964): 85-87.

"Film Costs Will Soar 36% in 1984", *Variety,* 15 February 1984.

Film Daily. 3 November 1936, p. 6.

Frohman, Daniel. "Do Motion Pictures Mean the Death of Drama?" *The Theatre,* 22 (December 1915): 310.

————. "Movies and the Theatre." *Woman's Home Companion,* November 1913.

Gillette, William. "The Illusion of the First Time in Acting." In *Papers on Acting.* Edited by Brander Matthews. New York: Dramatic Museum of Columbia University, 1915.

Gray, Paul. "Stanislavski and America: A Critical Chronology." *Tulane Drama Review,* 9, No. 2 (Winter 1964): 21-60.

Griffith, D.W. "A Poet Who Writes on Motion Picture Film." *The Theatre,* 19 (June 1914): 311-16.

————. "Don't Blame the Movies!" *Motion Picture Magazine,* 31, (July 1926).

————. "Pictures vs. One-Night Stands." *Independent,* 11 December 1916: 447-48.

————. "What I Demand of Movie Stars." *Moving Picture Classic,* 3 (February 1917).

Gussow, Mel. "Dustin Hoffman's *Salesman.*" *New York Times Magazine* 18 March 1984.

Hoffman, Theodore. "TDR Comment: Stanislavski Triumphant." *Tulane Drama Review,* 9, No. 1 (Fall 1964): 9-18.

Howard, William K. "Stage and Screen Acting are Almost Alike." *New York World Telegram,* 21 January 1939.

Isaacs, Edith J. R. "Type Casting: Eighth Deadly Sin." *Theatre Arts Monthly,* 17 (February 1933): 131-38.

Janney, Russell. "Richard Boleslawski." [sic] *New York Herald Tribune,* 31 January 1937, 33.

Kazan, Elia. "Look, There's The American Theatre." *Tulane Drama Review* 9, No. 2 (Winter 1964): 61-83.

Kerr, Walter F. "Acting Techniques Discussed." *New York Herald Tribune,* 17 August 1957, 4.

Kirby, Michael. "On Acting and Not Acting." *The Drama Review,* 16, No. 1 (March 1972): 3-15.

Knox, Alexander. "Acting and Behaving." *Hollywood Quarterly* [now *Film Quarterly*], 1, No. 3 (Spring 1946): 260-69.

Krutch, Joseph W. "On Adequate Acting." *The Nation,* 10 January 1934, 56.

————. "On Make Believe and Acting." *The Nation,* 30 March 1927.

Larrabee, Eric. Review of *Theory of Film* by Siegfried Kracauer. *Harper's,* January 1961, 31.

Lewis, Robert. "A Point of View and a Place to Practice." *Theatre Arts Monthly,* April 1960, 62-64.

_____. "Would You Please Talk to Those People?" *Tulane Drama Review*, 9, No. 2 (Winter 1964): 97-113.

Lewisohn, Ludwig. "An American Art Theatre—Why Not?" *Theatre Magazine*, August 1923, 9.

Lowell, Sondra. "About Those Strasberg Tapes." *Los Angeles Times*, Part V, 12 November 1983, sec. 5.

MacGowan, Kenneth. "And Again Repertory: The Moscow Art Theatre and Shakespeare Divide New York Honors." *Theatre Arts Magazine*, 7, No. 2, (April 1923): 89-104.

Mann, Paul. "Theory and Practice." *Tulane Drama Review*, 9, No.2 (Winter, 1964): 84-96.

Mansfield, Richard. "Concerning Acting." *The North American Theatre Review*, (September 1894): 337-40.

Matthews, Brander. "Are the Movies a Menace to the Drama?" *North American Review*, 205 (1917): 447-54.

McCormick, Lynde. "Robert Duvall," *American Film*, September 1981, 41-42.

Meisner, Sanford. "The Reality of Doing." *Tulane Drama Review*, 9, No. 1 (Fall 1964): 136-55.

Meyerhold, Vsevolod. "The Booth." Translated by Alexander Bakshy. *Drama*, No. 26 (May 1917): 203-216, and No. 27 (August 1917): 425-47.

_____. "From *On the Theatre*." Translated by Nora Beeson. *Tulane Drama Review*, 4 (September 1959): 139-49.

Muni, Paul. "The Actor Plays His Part." *We Make the Movies*. Edited by Nancy Naumberg. New York: W.W. Norton, 1937.

Newsweek, 21 November 1936, 20.

New Theatre Magazine, November 1936, 34.

New York Dramatic Mirror, 26 January 1907, 3.

O'Malley, Suzanne. "Can the Method Survive the Madness?" *New York Times Magazine*, 7 October 1979, 32.

"Paul Orlenev and His Company of Russian Actors." *Theatre Magazine*, 5 (December 1905): xi.

Ouspenskaya, Maria. (Obit.) *New York Times*, 4 December 1949, 108.

Peck, Seymour. "The Temple of 'The Method.'" *New York Times Magazine*, 6 May 1956, 24.

Pichel, Irving. "Character, Personality and Image: A Note on Screen Acting." *Hollywood Quarterly* (now *Film Quarterly*), 2 (October 1946): 25-29.

Pudovkin, V.I. "The Actor's Work: Film v. Stage." Translated by V. Sonutchinsky. *Close Up*, 10, No.3 (September 1933): 227-34.

Rogoff, Gordon. "Lee Strasberg: Burning Ice." *Tulane Drama Review*, 9, No. 2 (Winter 1964): 131-54.

"Russian Artiste Becomes an American Star." *Theatre Magazine*, 7, (January 1907): 13.

Shaw, Bernard, and Archibald Henderson. "Drama, The Theatre, and The Films." *Fortnightly Review*, 122 (1924): 289-302.

Skinner, Otis. "An Actor's View of the Movie Menace." *North American Review*, 212 (1920): 387-92.

Soloviova, Vera. "The Reality of Doing." *Tulane Drama Review*, 9, No. 1 (Fall 1964): 136-55.

Stanislavski, Constantin. "The Art of the Actor and the Art of the Director." *Stanislavsky's Legacy*. Edited by Elizabeth Reynolds Hapgood. New York: Theatre Arts Books, 1958, pp.170-82.

_____. "Director and Actor at Work." Translated by Elizabeth Reynolds Hapgood. *Tulane Drama Review*, 9, No. 1 (Fall 1964): 57-62.

_____. "The Hard Job of Being an Actor." *Stanislavsky's Legacy*. Edited By Elizabeth Reynolds Hapgood. New York: Theatre Arts Books, 1958, pp. 9-12.

_____. "Types of Actors." *Stanislavsky's Legacy*. Edited by Elizabeth Reynolds Hapgood. New York: Theatre Arts Books, 1958, pp.13-19.

_____. "Why and When Play Melodrama." *Stanislavsky's Legacy*. Edited by Elizabeth Reynolds Hapgood. New York: Theatre Arts Books, 1958, pp. 138-52.

Strasberg, Lee. "Acting." In the *New Encyclopaedia Britannica*, 15th ed, Macropaedia.

———. "Acting and the Training of the Actor." In *Producing the Play*. Edited by John Gassner. New York: Crown Publishers, 1941, 128-62.

———. "The Magic of Meyerhold." *New Theatre*, 1, (September 1934).

———. "Strasberg vs. TDR." *Tulane Drama Review*, 11, No. 1 (Fall 1966): 234-39.

———. "View for the Studio." *New York Times*, 2 September 1956, sec. 2, p.1.

———. "Working with Live Material." Interview by Richard Schechner. *Tulane Drama Review*, 9, No.1 (Fall 1964): 117-35.

Talma, François Joseph. "Reflections on Acting." In *Papers on Acting*. Edited by Brander Matthews. New York: Hill and Wang, 1958.

Theatre Magazine, 7 (March 1907): 72.

Towse, J. Rankin. *New York Evening Post*, 30 January 1923.

Vakhtangov, Eugene. "Eugene Vakhtangov: 1883-1922." (Excerpts from his diary.) *Theatre Arts*, 20 (September 1936): 679.

———. "Fantastic Realism." In *Directors on Directing*. Rev. ed., edited by Toby Cole and Helen K. Chinoy. Indianapolis: Bobbs-Merrill Co., 1953; 1963, 185-91.

Ward, Robert. "Rod Steiger, Hollywood's Last Angry Man." *American Film*, February, 1982.

Wasserman, Debbi. "Developing an American Acting Style." *New York Theatre Review*, February 1978, 5-9.

Whitney, P. "Expressing Movie Emotion." *Vanity Fair*, October 1919.

Willis, Ronald A. "The American Lab Theatre." *Tulane Drama Review*, 9, No. 1 (Fall 1964): 112-16.

Young, Stark. "A Note: Moving Picture Acting." *New Republic*, 72, (1932): 150-51.

Zolotow, Maurice. "The Stars Rise Here." *Saturday Evening Post*, 18 May 1957, 86.

Reviews

Review of *Coming Home. Variety*, 17 February 1978.

Review of *Garden of Allah. Daily Variety*, October 31, 1936, p.3.

Review of *Heaven's Gate. Variety*, 26 November 1980.

Review of *The Late Mrs. Cheney. The Hollywood Reporter*, 15 February 1937, 3.

Review of *On Golden Pond. Variety*, 17 September 1980.

Review of *Raging Bull. Wall Street Journal*, 28 November 1980, 40.

Unpublished Materials

Actors Studio. Membership List (1984).

———. Golden Globe Award File on Studio Membership (1984).

———. Academy Award Winners and Nominees From Studio Membership (1984).

———. Emmy Award Winners and Nominees From Studio Membership (1984).

———. Deceased Membership Award List (n.d.).

———. Obie Award Winners from Studio Membership. (n.d.).

———. "Actors Studio: Brief History," 1983 (2 pp.).

Ashby, Clifford Charles. "Realistic Acting and the Advent of the Group in America: 1889-1922." Ph.D. diss., Stanford, 1963.

Boleslavski, Richard. "The Creative Theatre." Lectures translated by Michael Barroy (1923). Typescript in Theatre Collection, New York Public Library. Available on microfilm.

Brumm, Beverly M. "A Survey of Professional Acting Schools in New York City: 1870-1970." Ph.D. diss., New York University, 1973.

Buttons, Red. Interview with author. 13 February, 1984.

Hardy, Michael C. "The Theatre of Richard Boleslavsky." Ph.D. diss., University of Michigan, 1971.

Hetler, Louis. "The Influence of the Stanislavsky Theories of Acting on the Teaching of Acting in the United States." Ph.D. diss., Denver, 1957.

Scharfenberg, Jean. "Lee Strasberg: Teacher." Ph.D. diss., Wisconsin, 1963.

Strasberg, Lee. Lectures at the Lee Strasberg Theatre Institute, Los Angeles, California, Summer 1973.

"20/20" Feature segment on Paul Newman and Joanne Woodward. ABC-TV, 29 March 1984. Transcript available from ABC-TV, New York.

Index